CHASING AFTER THE WIND

KERRYN REDPATH

Chasing After the Wind

All Rights Reserved

Copyright © 2017 Kerryn Redpath

Reproduction in any manner, in whole or in part, in English or any other language, or otherwise, without the written permission of the copyright holder is prohibited

For information address: kerryn@kerrynredpath.com.au

First Published in 2017

ISBN: 978-0-6480021-7-8

Published by The Mickie Dalton Foundation
NSW
Australia

<u>www.mickiedaltonfoundation.com</u>

Dedication

I dedicate this book to

my beautiful 'miracle' children,

Kyle, Stefan and Phoebe.

You continually amaze and inspire me.

Dream big!

Love always,

Mum

Cover photo by Dalton Portella

Titled "Fury VII"

The ocean off Montauk, New York,

during a thunderstorm.

www.daltonportella.com

I have chosen the image of a thunderstorm as I see a parallel between lightening and drug use. From a distance both can look attractive, and yet to find yourself in the middle of either, can be dangerous even deadly.

"Learn from other's mistakes. You can't live long enough to make them all yourself."

Eleanor Roosevelt

Disclaimers

In writing this book, I have been faithful to my memory. The opinions and recollections expressed are my own, but I accept my subjects may have a different view or remember things differently.

At my discretion throughout the book, I have changed parties' names to protect their identities. Where I have used parties' real names, I have done so either with their express permission or in circumstances where their names are already in the public domain. It is my hope that my use of the names of those whose lives have tragically been lost, help serve as a warning to others about the potential dangers of alcohol and other drug use.

The information given in this book is not medical advice and should not be relied on in this way. Individuals wanting medical advice on any of the issues mentioned should consult a health professional.

All information has been researched and represented as identified at the time of research.

All links used were available during the writing of this book which covered the period October 2015 to October, 2017.

ENDORSEMENTS

... a compelling, must read...

Kerryn's compelling book "Chasing After the Wind" is hard to put down. It depicts not only her own personal story of life threatening drug addiction but the heartache of living with a partner battling addiction. Combined with an educational component on drugs and alcohol and an appendix of helpful and relevant articles, it is passionately produced and a much needed weapon in the war against substance abuse.

I have been privileged to witness fifteen of Kerryn's presentations in and around Adelaide, predominantly in secondary schools. Her professional delivery, well researched material, integrated with anecdotal accounts of her own personal experiences, completely captivates her audience, leaving them with abundant information and a clear insight into the reality of drug and alcohol use and abuse.

I highly recommend this book be made available to young people everywhere and in fact to any age group as this is not only a powerful story, but a great educational tool. I also strongly endorse Kerryn's Drug and Alcohol Awareness Education presentation to secondary schools, youth groups and public or corporate sectors. Drug and alcohol use is an issue that affects people of all age groups and demographics.

'Chasing After the Wind' is a real pager turner and it will save lives.

Patricia Taylor
Author 'Someone to Watch Over Me'

... Compelling in its frailties, its courage, its despair,

There are some questions that don't have answers. One of them is: How is it that Kerryn Redpath is still alive? There are other questions that do have answers, like: Why is Kerryn Redpath still alive? The answer to that, as you will find when you read her book, Chasing After the Wind, is simple: to share her story with as many people as she can in the hope that it will save lives.

I am not alone in saying Kerryn is an inspiration. I knew it the first day I met her at the school we both worked at. It wasn't hard to detect. It never is when someone wears their heart on their sleeve the way Kerryn does. You see, Kerryn loves people and she loves life. She told me then, 15 years ago now, that she was a reformed drug addict and how it had left her permanently damaged but it wasn't until some years later that I came to learn the full extent of her past addiction and the toll it had taken. It was then that I understood that her love of people and life stemmed from having been so close to losing her own life and being forever lost to the people she cared for the most.

When Kerryn asked me how she should write her book, I told her to be herself. And that's what she has done. The voice you hear as you read these pages is Kerryn's – heartfelt, heart-wrenching, honest, driven, compelling. Compelling in its frailties, its courage, its despair, its conviction and its love. It needs to be all these things because the message that is being delivered demands it and, as you will most certainly discover, Kerryn is the ideal messenger.

Carolyn Hastings
BAppSc(SpPath)
Melbourne, Australia
carolynh@aasp.net.au

… highly recommended, authentic …

I have known Kerryn for over twenty years and whilst her story is not my own we lived and moved in the same circles, our children were friends and in particular her second son and my son were best of friends and still are to this day.

I've watched Kerryn and David bring up their children from pre-primary through to adulthood. Kerryn was always the more upfront of the two, whilst David was clearly a loving father; he tended to be in the background. As a bystander my blinkers were on and I didn't see what was in front of me. As so often is the case with family secrets minimizing personal struggles was prevalent. It was years before Kerryn opened up to me about her past addiction and David's ongoing addiction and the subsequent struggles, loneliness and isolation she felt.

It's for these reasons that I highly recommend this book for its authenticity, thoroughness and relevance to people struggling in the area of addiction, whether directly or indirectly. Abuse and addictions are not merely family problems, they are society problems and Kerryn's heart in sharing her story is to impact the next generation so that they don't make the same mistakes that she did. This story *is also for those struggling with living with an addict, understanding what is happening and knowing that help is there and even more than that – there is hope.*

Judy Young (Oakleigh South)

… No, not our Kerryn …

"As we celebrated our daughter Kerryn's birthday last year, memories of another birthday many years ago came flooding back - a birthday we were told she would never live to see. A few months before her 26th birthday, she had been admitted to hospital gravely ill. We were told by her doctor, Dr. Suzanne Crowe and her specialist Professor Barry Firkin, who had admitted her earlier on that day, that her heart and kidneys were so badly damaged that she could not survive the night.

This shocking news was repeated as we pleaded with them to help her. In disbelief we listened to the reasons for her illness - she had been using drugs and alcohol!!! No, not our Kerryn! Although we were so shocked and distressed by this news, it became a secondary problem to be thought about later, as she battled through the night and miraculously through the following days ...

Today, we are both so proud of how Kerryn not only turned her life around many years ago, but works hard in her effort to use her knowledge and experience to warn others of the dangers of drug and alcohol use and abuse and also gives of her time to help people battling addiction.

Kerryn's very grateful parents Annette and Harry

... should be read by all ...

This is a most compelling story which, in the context of tragedies associated with drug addiction, has a happy outcome. In her story, Kerryn describes her inexorable spiral downwards from a normal, loving adolescent, into the dark world of drugs and in particular, heroin addiction. She was one of the lucky ones. The dice never seemed to point absolutely directly at her. Her drug crazed world with heroin and other drugs was brought to a crashing demise with the development of a severe infection (hepatitis B), which in turn led to a rare complication associated with this virus - polyarteritis nodosum. Death seemed inevitable, but with the intervention of appropriate medical therapy she rather remarkably survived. To this day she remains well physically, over 30 years after her almost cataclysmic demise.

This is a story that should be read by all - young and old, parents, teenagers and current or past addicts of all persuasions. It is written in a simple matter-of-fact style and includes very relevant information. It is a story that should be especially read by all teenagers in their passage through the years of life, where they are most frequently brought in touch with the abhorrent world of drug addiction, in all its forms. This story strongly underscores the need for living a life with goals or dreams that can give a person purpose and hope and provide the will and stability to reject this seductive lifestyle. Kerryn is a lucky one - she survived. This story is perhaps redolent of many, but nevertheless it is very compelling and provides a stark and sobering glimpse of the world of drug addiction.

Associate Professor Peter Ryan   2017

CONTENTS

PART I

Introduction	1
1. Beginnings	4
2. Kathmandu	15
3. Home Again	20
4. The Downward Spiral	26
5. Think First	35
6. Hallucinogens	39
7. Wild Days	50
8. Terror	55
9. Repercussions	65
10. What will it take?	73
11. The Love of a Mother	80
12. Maternal Instincts	83
13. Living with the Enemy – Marijuana	100
14. Recollections and Regrets	117
15. The Other Side of the Story	122
16. The Drugs Triumph	125
17. Why?	142

PART II

18.	Hope	149
19.	Meth	151
19a.	A Tribute to Aaron	168
20.	Heroin (& other Opiates)	175
21.	MDMA – Ecstasy	182
22.	GHB & Ketamine	186
23.	New Psychoactive Substances (Synthetic Drugs)	192
24.	Alcohol	196
25.	What to do in an Emergency	206
26.	Who Benefits?	210
27.	Why Drugs or Alcohol?	214
28.	I Am Not My Mistakes	225
29.	Dream!	228
Finale - Placebo Town (Revisited) by David Redpath		233

PART III

Appendix - Related Articles	239
Student Feedback	262
References	265

Chasing After the Wind

Introduction

It is my deepest hope that the information, memories and real-life stories recorded in the following pages will inspire and empower others to follow their dreams and not follow the path that so often leads to destruction.

From the outset I want to make it clear that I have not set out to harm, ridicule, blame-shift or destroy the life of any particular person or persons. Addiction is a devastating affliction that destroys body, spirit, mind and soul. It changes people from normal loving, caring, functioning human beings into hollow souls driven by a mental, physical and emotional need to fill a void and in the process, tears apart families, friendships and communities; a shocking phenomenon plaguing families across this amazing yet weary planet.

Mine is just one such story and since publishing my own account in 2010 I have been driven by the voice in my head to tell the other side of the story, the one of living with an addict. But that will come later. Of course this is just one of the consequences of the choice I made to use drugs and I am not solely basing these recollections around one topic.

In reference to the 'blame-shifting' comment, I must add that I absolutely carry my share of blame, but I have also learnt to forgive not only all others, but myself for the stupid choices I made and the crazy, desperate and at times inappropriate way I handled certain situations. Forgiveness is a huge part of addiction recovery.

My motivation for penning these pages is my deep and heartfelt desire to warn anyone considering entering the dark world of drugs, about the horror that so often follows such a decision. These words of warning come from one who has been there, has paid the price and still pays the price today. I am certain that any other person who has travelled this soul destroying road would also wish to warn those who may be tempted to follow.

Another driving force behind this account is the fact that over the last year or so my mind has suddenly become filled with further memories of that time, memories I had pushed down so far, too painful to muse over. But now my mind was so filled with the echoes of the past that I felt compelled to put pen to paper and get them out of my head, and I began to write. A very therapeutic process! My time of deep healing had come.

So there they sat, out of my head and sprawled across the pages of an exercise book for months, when I began to realise that these words could well serve as a warning to others and so the next chapter of my story begins.

PART I

1

Beginnings

"Is this existence a swirling vortex?"

Slumped on the floor in the corner of the room, with my two precious young children innocently sleeping, my head was numb, tears flowing freely as I felt totally alone in a world few knew about. As one who had recklessly followed the crowd into the party scene years earlier and barely survived drug addiction, I was now free from drugs and moving forward from my past. But the past had pursued me into the present as the man I had married continued to battle addiction.

Together we had once lived life as if there were no tomorrow, partying hard and taking risks so shocking, that the slightest memory of them, even now, causes me to shudder and leaves a sick, empty feeling in the pit of my stomach.

Now, there was no one I could turn to. The feeling of hopelessness overwhelmed me as I allowed the pain to erupt from deep within, in a gush of sobbing…

~~~~~~~~~~

Substance use and abuse is nothing new. For centuries men and women have used alcohol and other drugs to alter their natural state of mind and loosen their inhibitions as a form of relaxation, celebration and medication. Sounds good doesn't it? But it's far from good. As the incidence of drug and alcohol use among people of all age groups and demographics surges across the world, we are increasingly faced with the devastating impact this has on the lives of so many. I fully understand the desire most of us have to fit in with our peers and also the wish to have fun; there's nothing wrong with wanting to get some enjoyment out of life. However, as I'm sure we all know, the use of alcohol and other drugs can and often does turn to tragedy.

Although much of my own disastrous story took place many years ago, the shocking side effects of drug and alcohol use and abuse on a worldwide scale, has not altered.

As someone who has seen, lived through and only just survived so much of the devastation caused by drug and alcohol use, in plain simple terms let me just say … Drugs destroy lives!

~~~~~~~~~~

To summarise a little of my story, I entered the world quite uneventfully in a busy inner-city hospital in Richmond, a suburb of Melbourne, Australia. Blessed at birth with a strong, healthy body, I grew up in a 'normal' loving family. I was a middle child and the only girl with two brothers. I spent my early years living in and out of the lives of the local neighbourhood kids, occupying our time with numerous outdoor activities and, long before the 'age of technology', using our imagination to entertain ourselves.

From as young as I can remember I loved horses and for years I begged Mum and Dad to buy me a pony, until finally at the age of fifteen my parents bought me my first horse; a handsome chestnut gelding I named Tokay. I did a lot of pleasure riding but I also joined pony clubs (and later adult riding club), where I was coached to improve my riding, jumping and horsemanship in general. I began competing at gymkhanas, shows and dressage events and so began a life-long obsession with these beautiful creatures.

In my early teenage years, Dad also bought a small speed boat and he and my brothers and I all learnt to water ski. We spent so many weekends over the long, hot Melbourne Summers, lapping up the sunshine at various lakes and beaches, flying across the water, with the wind in our hair and without a care in the world.

I have many wonderful childhood memories; in particular our Christmas holidays spent camping on Ulupna Island on the Murray River. We swam, skied and swung into the water from 'Tarzan ropes' for so many hours each day that our skin would wrinkle. As I recall these times, I can still feel the burning heat of the hot sand on the soles of my feet and the painful sting of sunburn on my shoulders. Apart from our many encounters with spiders and a few with snakes, the scariest memory I have of the Murray River days, was having to go to the dingy, makeshift 'bush dunny'[1], with its hessian walls and the hundreds of spiders that my imagination created. Sitting around a crackling fire on the beach and gazing into the brilliant starry heavens was often the peaceful ending to a long, active day. All of these things added to the excitement of our summer break. In later years, we changed our holiday destination to the Hume Weir Holiday Homes near Albury in NSW. Life was a little more civilized there, but we enjoyed many of the same activities plus nightly tennis matches.

While I was in senior school, the parents of my best friend, Vicki, bought a property at Pine Bay[2] and they very generously invited me to move my horse there with Vicki's horse. Pine Bay is a beautiful little seaside town on the Mornington Peninsula in Victoria with two main beaches and a picturesque golf course with breath-taking views over Westernport Bay. Over the next few years I spent almost every weekend with Vicki and her family on their cosy 'weekender - hobby farm'. We discovered countless amazing horse-riding trails and spent hours each weekend and during school holidays, riding and exploring all over the beautiful countryside.

---

[1] Toilet
[2] Fictional name of a real town.

Back then this little town was a bit of a hidden 'gem' with its 'front beach' and 'back beach' and at times we headed to the spectacular back-beach where we rode along the golden sand or swam in the crashing waves on our rather energetic horses. Over time we also became close to many of the locals and gradually Vicki and I became part of the local scene.

So I was very fortunate. My weekdays naturally, were spent going to school and weekends were spent horse-riding, water-skiing or just hanging out with friends. We weren't overly wealthy; Mum and Dad worked hard for what we had, but in my teenage years, like so many others, I started to take some risks.

The path to addiction so often begins with the lure of seemingly innocent risk-taking, as teens, thinking they are indestructible, start to 'cross the line', with no comprehension of the slippery slope these apparently minor actions can set in motion.

The first risk I took was one of these 'harmless' little acts of daring as one day Vicki and I sneaked some of her father's cigars and took them out to the horse agistment property where we hid in a stable and lit up. What followed was much coughing and spluttering, as we enjoyed, not the foul taste of the cigars, but that sweet taste of rebellion. And that is where it all began.

Young and naïve and quite shy as a teenager, I just wanted to 'fit in' and like so many others, rather than being an individual and thinking for myself, I blindly followed what many of my peers were doing. Next it was cigarettes, just a puff here and there, but before long smoking these insipid little sticks of poison had become a daily habit. Then came the alcohol, 'everyone else' was doing it. It all just seemed like a bit of fun and as I was under age and my parents were unaware, the lure was even greater.

When I was growing up the nature of addiction of any kind was a matter rarely discussed in families or in the media. Most popular magazines of the day portrayed the family image of a smiling housewife and a happy hard-working husband with the 2.5 children, living in a shiny home with a cat, a dog and a white picket fence. If a family member had a drug or alcohol problem, it was usually denied and carefully hidden from other family members, friends and neighbours as we lived in a very private culture. This combined with a total lack of understanding; shame and ignorance were the driving forces behind the denial. It's not that different today as addiction is often seen as a lack of control or a weakness and a source of shame to those affected, which is the case for some. But overall there is far more understanding of this as a form of illness or a health issue and a devastating 'disease' of our society that often requires prolonged treatment in order to overcome.

Sadly, it's a well-known fact that many people, who use drugs and alcohol, are actually traumatised souls who are self-medicating in an attempt to 'numb out' some form of emotional pain or possibly a mental health issue like depression or anxiety etc. This is NOT the answer! If a person has suffered some kind of trauma or mental health issue and they self-medicate with drugs or alcohol in an attempt to block out pain, they have then opened the door to a whole new level of trauma, multiplying the problem. (See Chapter 27 for more on this topic)

Of course this is not the case for every drug or alcohol user. Many, like was the case for me, are just wanting to 'fit in' and follow their peers down this risky path and in the process, become part of the cultural epidemic of substance use and abuse.

Another devastating phenomenon plaguing this planet is the issue of prescription drug abuse with three main categories involved. Firstly, pharmaceutical opioids, which were developed to be used as painkillers; secondly, benzodiazepines (benzos) which are used as 'minor tranquilizers' and are regularly prescribed for anxiety or sleep problems; and thirdly, stimulant drugs which are often prescribed for ADHD or narcolepsy (sleep disorder) etc.

All three of these types of prescription drugs can be addictive. As a consequence there are numerous people who begin using one of these medications to ease a genuine health issue, but then go on to develop dependence to the drug they have been prescribed.

Unfortunately there are also those who use these drugs for 'recreational' purposes which can easily lead to dependence or overdose. Lastly, and very sadly, many people take prescription pain killers, tranquilizers or stimulants to self-medicate in an attempt to 'block out' emotional pain and tragically become addicted.

Regardless of the motive, this is a massive and potentially deadly issue involving millions of people right across the globe; the latest example being the recent tragic death of the world famous musician, [3]Prince who died as the result of an 'accidental' overdose of opioid pain killers. According to reports more people lose their lives every year to prescription drug overdose than to all illicit drug overdoses combined. "Contrary to popular mythology, prescription drugs are more lethal than illegal or street drugs. Prescription drug abuse and addiction kills far

---

[3] *A medical examination has concluded that Prince died of an accidental overdose of pain medication. The medicine, fentanyl, is an opioid and is* **one of the strongest painkillers available.** *Fentanyl is prescribed for cancer treatment, but it's also being made illicitly and sold on the streets, delivering a super high and far too often, death. Prince had been suffering from a bad hip -- and some who knew him said he had been addicted to pain meds for some time.* *** *CNN News Report June 3, 2016.*
http://www.cnn.com/2016/06/03/health/prince-death-opioid-overdose/ By Faith Karimi and Sara Sidner - CNN - Jun 3, 2016

more people in the U.S. every year than all illegal drugs combined."[4] [5]

But it is important to note that there is always hope!

~~~~~~~~~

At the age of eighteen and not long after I'd passed my driver's licence, a girlfriend and I headed off for a short holiday to Lorne, a beautiful coastal town South West of Melbourne. It was our first real taste of independence and Kathy and I revelled in the freedom of our summer getaway.

While we were in Lorne, we met a couple of guys who were surfers visiting Victoria from Western Australia and one night they offered me a 'joint' (marijuana). This involved just a few seconds that would combine to become one of the most defining moments in my life. I had never considered whether or not I would ever use drugs. Until this day I had hardly even seen an illicit drug, and to one who was now unwittingly crossing 'that line', it simply seemed like a bit of fun. I didn't feel particularly pressured by these guys, but by myself, as the words spinning in my head told me "It won't be cool to say no." However, as I look back it's clear to see that the prevalence of drug use

---

[4] https://www.psychologytoday.com/blog/wicked-deeds/201404/prescription-drugs-are-more-deadly-street-drugs - by **Scott Bonn, Ph.D. - Psychology today - April 18, 2014**

[5] https://www.theguardian.com/australia-news/2015/mar/21/prescription-drugs-involved-in-82-of-overdose-overdose-deaths-victoria-coroner-says - by Melissa Davey - The Guardian Australia - 2015

was rapidly increasing in this country, it just wasn't recognised as the huge problem that it is today. In light of this, combined with the shame and denial era we lived in, there was little or no drug & alcohol awareness education in schools, workplaces or in the media. In other words, teens growing up in my era were pretty naïve on the topic of substance use. I don't blame anyone for the absence of education; it just wasn't considered necessary back then.

But times have changed. Today schools and workplaces across the country do offer ample Drug & Alcohol Awareness education ranging from Government programs implemented by staff, to visiting guest speakers from a wide range of backgrounds. These programs are not just used to fill in a bit of spare time. They are seen as a necessity to protect, inform and help educate students and employees with the aim of avoiding at best and minimising at least, the devastation and destruction caused by illicit and addictive substance use to individuals, families and communities right across the world.

So, totally uninformed and ignorant of any negative side to marijuana, I joined in and smoked my first joint. Little did I know, this was to be just the beginning and gradually I began to slide into a lifestyle where smoking marijuana was becoming 'the norm'.

It was at this time that my friend Vicky and I had begun to plan a trip overseas. We had both been working for a while and saving up for our adventure. At first, it was to be to New Zealand, but then Vicki was inspired by another friend's travels to India and Asia and our plans were changed.

The idea was to fly up to Kathmandu in Nepal and to then gradually work our way back down through Asia to Malaysia, Indonesia and then back home again. We had allowed six to eight months for our big adventure and at last, the time had arrived.

2

Kathmandu

"Are we colour living in contrast?"

After months of planning and anticipation, hours of flying, a stopover in Bangkok and again briefly in India, Vicki and I finally arrived in Kathmandu. We were greeted by a surge of moist, hot air as we descended from the plane onto the tarmac. It was 1976 and security was pretty slack, so the check-out was quick and we soon found ourselves wandering around the streets of this amazing ancient city. One of the first smells we recognised as we meandered along was the strong, pungent but familiar aroma of marijuana smoke. My fateful trip to Kathmandu had begun.

Our first place of accommodation was in a little lane named Pig Alley, in a run down two-storey, mud brick building. It was pretty rough, but fascinating, just what we Aussie backpackers were looking for. After a couple of days we moved to another place, which was even more dodgy, but closer to the centre of town. It was in the middle of Freak Street, where all sorts of activities took place right outside all night, every night. This building had such a low roof that being reasonably tall I had to duck my head to pass under the ceiling beams.

We did some normal touristy things during the day, but most nights we seemed to end up in some sleazy 'smoking den' where pipes, bongs and joints were passed around and much hashish was smoked. The dens had a feel all of their own, with their colourful eastern-style fabrics draped about, with visitors sitting on cushions scattered around small tables on the floor. The lighting was dim and the room constantly filled with a thick haze of smoke, as we gradually numbed our minds with hash. Being young and naïve we had no concept of just how risky this behaviour was. We were healthy, youthful and carefree and just 'living the dream'. But in reality we were living in a world we really didn't know, taking crazy risks, totally oblivious to any potential dangers that may have come our way.

~~~~~~~~~~

Some years after our trip to Nepal, I read a book on the story of Charles Sobrhaj. Sobrhaj, nick-named the bikini killer, had been a psychopathic serial killer who was roaming around India, Nepal and South East Asia, preying on Western tourists during the 70's. According to my calculations he was in the vicinity of Nepal and possibly not far from us at the time that we were there. Not only were we overly innocent about meeting strangers on our journey (we thought everyone was nice), but we were often so stoned, that we would not have been able to think clearly had we found ourselves in a threatening situation. This is typical behaviour for a young person with an immature brain (A topic I will touch on later). Thankfully he was eventually caught and convicted of his heinous crimes. In the book that I read about Sobrhaj, the author, who had interviewed him in prison said, "Despite knowing the horrific, murderous crimes Sobrhaj had committed, I could not help but be drawn in by his incredible charisma" (paraphrased). If Vicki and I had met with Sobrhaj while in Nepal, I'm sure we would have been history.

~~~~~~~~~~

Then, without warning, my adventure began to take a turn.

Within a week of arriving in Nepal, I became violently ill with vomiting and diarrhoea. It was fortunate that the bath was right next to the toilet as I was able to sit on the loo while I threw up repeatedly into the bath! After a few days of this, and despite how I was feeling, we journeyed on, travelling by bus around the treacherous, winding mountain roads to Pokhara; a magnificent, picturesque part of Nepal where we could easily see the peaks of the Himalayas early in the morning before they disappeared into the cloud cover. We truly were in another world. But I was becoming weaker. I pushed on thinking that I probably just had a bad dose of dysentery and treated it as such. Although I was seriously 'unwell', I kept hoping that it would pass and we continued on. Being in this beautiful town was like taking a step back in time and with my health deteriorating, I tried to make the most of it. After a week in Pokhara, we arrived back in Kathmandu, stayed a few more days and then caught a flight to Rangoon, the Capital of Burma (now known as Myanmar).

The next episode of our adventure was to travel by boat down the Irrawaddy River from Mandalay to Pagan. We caught a rattling, over-crowded train from Rangoon to Mandalay, spent a day there and then boarded the boat to begin our journey along the river to Pagan. This boat was actually some big, old ship and we paid for a shared cabin. Meanwhile, every inch of the deck was covered with locals who claimed a small space and sat or laid in that space for the entire voyage. Along the river, the towns and the people we passed were fascinating.

At each town, hordes of people lined the shore next to the ship hoping to sell their fruit, vegetables and wares to the passengers. But for me the whole journey was heart breaking, as in the midst of the extreme heat and humidity, my illness laid me useless. About mid journey our weary old ship ran aground and we were stuck in the one place for a whole day until the tide had risen enough for another passing ship to nudge us off the river's floor. I felt sooo sick!

We finally arrived in Pagan. It was a small but beautiful village with horse and buggy transport, dirt roads and gorgeous bamboo and timber huts. I did my best to enjoy this amazing part of the world, but it was there in Pagan, in the middle of one night, that I experienced my first episode of delirium. I had woken up feeling really weird and clumsily struggled out of bed to go to the toilet. By now I was totally confused and disoriented and I sat on the ground and leant against a palm tree with my head spinning. I don't know how long I stayed there, but I knew things were not good. By this point I realised that my illness was pretty serious and as painful and disappointing as it was, I knew that I needed to head back home. I figured that if I wasn't going to survive, it would be better to die in Australia, rather than have my body flown home from Burma. What a bummer! I had planned six to eight months of travel and only lasted about a month. Sadly, I left Vicki behind to continue 'our' trip alone and flew back to Singapore.

My illness seemed to come in waves, so I had moments when I could function reasonably well. I was fortunate while in Singapore to meet an English guy, who showed me around for a few days, before catching my connecting flight back to the 'Land of Oz'.

3

Home Again

"Having been plucked, roasted & ground"

I arrived back in Melbourne to be greeted by my family and my boyfriend I had left behind. I saw my doctor who assumed that I had contracted a severe dose of dysentery and prescribed medication to ease the symptoms. After a few weeks I began to feel much better and although totally disappointed about my abruptly ended travels, I resumed living my normal life.

I was now nineteen and having worked an office job for a few years I decided it was time to spread my wings. I packed my bags, left my family home and moved out. I headed to my favourite hangout, *Pine Bay, where I had found a bungalow to rent from a lovely older lady. Daisy was a tiny lady who had been widowed for many years and she became like another mother to me, cooking for me and fussing over me. We shared many hours deep in conversation as she told me about her life and family and the years gone by.

One day, about three weeks after my return I was asked to help round up some cattle on horseback. Having ridden horses for years, I jumped at the opportunity. I saddled up one of Vicki's horses (my thoroughbred would have been too crazy) and joined Jack and Rachel early in the morning to begin the round-up.

Jack was Rachel's father and a real personality in the township. He was a ruggedly handsome man with a shock of dark hair swept back from his face. Jack had worked for years as a professional fisherman and later drove the pilot boat out to the tankers when they were entering or leaving Western Port Bay. But Jack's greatest love was for his three children and he showed this by joining them in all of their leisure pursuits.

Rachel was a slim, attractive young woman with long, dark hair. She was an extremely gifted horse rider and excelled in every discipline of the equestrian field, from dressage to showing and jumping and was even 'Female Jockey of the Year' at one time.

We herded the cattle across a few paddocks and then slowed to a walk and moved them quietly out onto the road, heading in towards the Pine Bay township. It was a beautiful, crisp morning and all was going well until suddenly, a motorbike came flying around the bend toward us. The cattle instantly took fright and spun around, charging back in our direction. With the whole herd racing straight at us, my horse freaked out and spun on the spot, losing her footing on the bitumen. She crashed to the ground crushing my left leg under her full weight. An agonising pain shot from my foot up the length of my leg as I fought to hold back tears. I knew something was broken.

After a very bumpy ride to the nearest doctor, in Hastings, my injured leg was x-rayed revealing a 'Pots Fracture' just above the ankle; in other words both the Tibia and Fibula were broken and I was told my leg would be in plaster for the next six to eight weeks.

My car at the time was an automatic and I was lucky it was my left leg that was broken as I was still able to drive. I continued to live in Pine Bay hopping around on my crutches feeling quite well, until about six weeks after arriving back from Nepal when I awoke in the middle of the night in a complete delirium, totally unaware of where I was. By morning the delirium had passed but I was not well. A girlfriend took me to Frankston Hospital, where I waited for several hours in the casualty ward with my face bright red and my tongue coated white. I felt like I was dying. It was a Saturday and they were busy and I guess not expecting any exotic diseases to appear. I was finally seen by a doctor, had a blood test and was sent home. I went back to my family home in Moorabbin. No results were ever forwarded from that blood test.

Once home my condition worsened. My family doctor made a home visit and this time diagnosed me with acute malaria and called an ambulance to have me rushed straight to Fairfield Infectious Diseases Hospital.

I was admitted into an isolation ward, where my room was like a six-sided 'cell' with barred windows. I was not allowed to leave the room and any visitors had to 'gown and mask up', before entering the room, because of the high risk of infection.

The next few weeks were just a blur. I have small windows of memory such as when my mum, who visited every day, told me that they had finally formally diagnosed me with 'Salmonella Para Typhoid A'. My earliest memories of that time consist of feelings of extreme heat, extreme cold and my body being flopped back and forward as I was being sponged down. I was so close to death with my life just hanging in the balance. There was no sure cure for typhoid other than antibiotics and continually trying to keep me cool. I remember one instance when the nurses told me that I had been burning up with fever, but as my body was fighting it I felt freezing cold. In an attempt to bring my extreme fever down, they tricked me by offering to give me a warm sponge which I agreed to. Instead, they gave me an icy cold sponge and in my delirious state, I believed it to be warm.

When the delirium had finally passed and I was heading out of danger, I recall looking out my window toward a huge palm tree, which reminded me of the tropical land I had recently left. I dreamed of being back there with Vicki, experiencing all of the awesome new sights and cultures instead of being trapped in this small, depressing prison-like cell. Although I was happy for Vicki, the letters and postcards I received from her only magnified these emotions.

Some years later when talking to my mum about my five-week stint in Fairfield Hospital, mum being very surprised, corrected me – I had been in there for ten weeks! I was stunned, but the dates she related proved her correct. I had been so sick that I had lost five weeks of my life. I had actually had my Typhoid vaccination before heading overseas, but I had contracted another strain of Typhoid, (para-typhoid) which apparently the shots did not cover.

Until this illness struck, I had been perfectly healthy throughout my life. It was revealed by doctors that I probably contracted this disease by eating food that had been handled by a para-typhoid carrier. In retrospect I realised that after smoking 'weed', which not only affects your thought process, but also leads to intense food cravings, aka 'the munchies'[6]. Vicki and I would

---

[6] *In 2015, scientists discovered that certain neurons at the base of the brain increased appetite when activated by THC.*

The research revealed that CB1 receptors flick a switch in the brain that induces this group of neurons to secrete a substance that makes the marijuana user hungry.

"Using cannabis also stimulates the production of ghrelin the 'hunger hormone', which increases your appetite," Professor Copeland said.

http://www.abc.net.au/news/health/2016-09-20/why-does-marijuana-give-you-the-munchies/7861526 by Yasmin Noone - ABC News - Sept 20, 2016 have been super careless about the condition of the café we chose and about the food we were eating. I remember well the dingy little café we visited in our haste to satisfy our hunger. In other words, had we not been stoned, we most likely would have selected a far more hygienic café to eat in. I am not trying to disrespect any of the beautiful Nepalese people. In a developing country this is simply a fact.

On Friday 13th August I 'celebrated' my 20th birthday in Fairfield Infectious Diseases Hospital with Salmonella Para Typhoid 'A' and a broken leg.

4

The Downward Spiral

"In a place called Placebo Town"

Now aged twenty and having survived my fateful trip to Nepal, I headed back to *Pine Bay, where I moved from the bungalow I had been living in, into a rental property that I shared with one of the local girls. Meg was a lovely girl but she was really into partying and our little home soon became somewhat of a party house, regularly filled with friends, especially on a Friday and Saturday night after the local pub had closed. What seemed like a bit of fun at the time, I can now clearly see was the continuing of my life spiralling further out of control.

By this time the occasional smoke of a joint had well and truly progressed to daily smoking of bongs and cigarettes, and weekend binge drinking. The life I was now living was so far from the 'normal' quiet life I had previously known that it felt exciting as we headed down the slippery path that so many follow.

To a young person, this might all seem like a bit of fun, and of course at times it was, but believe me there were many times when I felt totally paranoid as my head was spinning after smoking weed or using other substances. I also witnessed numerous others freaking out as they battled with the distorted thoughts and images brought on by using various mind altering substances. We had all fallen for the lie that this was just a normal part of growing up. There is nothing normal about smoking bongs until you are too stoned to leave the house; until you are left so lethargic that you can't get off the couch; until you get the munchies that lead to eating so much revolting food that you feel sick. But this was "cool", we told ourselves. It made us better than those 'straight' people. These are the ridiculous thoughts you have when you are using drugs. And yet what could be so cool about it? It wasn't as if we were the first people to ever get stoned. Millions had done this before us. There is nothing new or cool about writing yourself off to the point that you can't leave the house. For me, when I did leave the house after a heavy dope smoking session, the beginnings of paranoia often set in as I was convinced people were watching me, and of course I was certain they all knew that I was stoned. What were we thinking?

The thing is, once you cross that line into the world of taking mind altering substances, usually beginning with marijuana, I believe you have unwittingly dropped your guard and it then becomes so easy to say "yes" and move on to the next drug. And naturally this usually means that you are now hanging around with others who also use drugs, which gives you easy access to a multitude of varying substances. And so begins the slippery slope that can lead to poly drug use and addiction. I realise that not everyone who smokes weed moves on to other drugs, but believe me pretty much everyone I know who ever used heroin, Ice, GHB or Ecstasy etc. began by smoking marijuana. As far as I am concerned, marijuana definitely is a 'gateway' drug.

Of course my anecdotal account is not sufficient evidence of this. On Thursday June 08, 2017, it was reported in the Daily Mail, UK that studies have "proven that cannabis does lead teenagers to harder drugs". See link below.[7]

I know there will be some people reading this thinking, "This is a joke. There's nothing wrong with having a bit of fun." And I get that attitude. I thought like that once, too. But over the years I have seen so much of the devastation of drug and alcohol use and abuse that I know what I am talking about. I sincerely hope these people will put those thoughts aside and read on.

---

[7] http://www.dailymail.co.uk/news/article-4582548/Proof-cannabis-DOES-lead-teenagers-harder-drugs.html?mc_cid=cfda696a4a&mc_eid=39df3c9d42#ixzz4lju5BS1g   By Steve Doughty & Ben Spencer 25/7/17 Daily Mail

A few realities:

1. *Crime* - *In a survey of adult male prisoners in 2001, the AIC's Drug Use Careers of Offenders (DUCO) study found that 62 percent of adult male prisoners reported being under the influence of alcohol or illegal drugs at the time of the offence that later resulted in their incarceration.*[8]

2. *Rehab* - *We have a shortage of rehabilitation facilities across this nation as waiting lists grow, with addicts desperate to overcome their addiction in an attempt to regain control of their lives... Sadly everyone who starts out using drugs for 'a bit of fun' thinks this will never happen to them!*[9]

3. *Family Violence* - *Studies show that alcohol and other drugs play a significant role in domestic violence incidents in this nation; The 2015 ADIVA study found that heavy binge drinking made domestic violence 6 times more likely, and the effects far more severe. A tragic statistic.*[10]

4. *Marijuana Stats* - *Studies have found that teens under the age of 17 who regularly smoke marijuana are seven times more likely to commit suicide and eight*

---

[8] http://www.aic.gov.au/media_library/publications/tandi_pdf/tandi439.pdf Aust Institute of Criminology May 2012

[9] http://www.smh.com.au/nsw/addicts-wait-months-for-treatment-as-ice-usage-soars-20150325-1m7c6c.html - Rachel Browne - The Sydney Morning Herald - March 25, 2015

[10] http://www.deakin.edu.au/about-deakin/media-releases/articles/study-shows-alcohol-and-drugs-play-significant-role-in-domestic-violence - Researchers from Deakin School of Psychology - December 15, 2016

times more likely to use other drugs. They are 60% less likely to finish high school, with an overall poor educational outcome.[11] *- (This study by researchers in Australia and New Zealand, is a meta-analysis of three previous long-running studies that included nearly 4,000 participants). The study was funded by the Australian Government National Health and Medical Research Council and reported on CBC News.*

5. *More Stats - Research in New Zealand has shown that regular smoking or using of marijuana can cause a young person's I.Q. to drop by 7-8 points! - When exploring the long term effects of marijuana use, Dr. Nora Volkow, director of the National Institute on Drug Abuse (NIDA), told the Associated Press, "I think this is the cleanest study I've ever read"*[12]

6. *Psychosis - "One of the things that's in the literature at the moment is that if you use cannabis, you double your risk of psychosis" - Prof. Murat Yousel - quote from Documentary, Living with the Enemy.*[13]

---

[11] http://www.dailymail.co.uk/sciencetech/article-2751914/Teenagers-smoke-cannabis-daily-60-likely-finish-school-likely-commit-suicide-experts-warn.html by Sarah Griffiths - Mailonline - updated Sept, 12, 2014

[12] http://healthland.time.com/2012/08/28/does-weekly-marijuana-use-by-teens-really-cause-a-drop-in-iq/ By Maia Slazavitz - TIME - August 28, 2012

[13]

www.monash.edu.au/research/people/profiles/profile.html?sid=4942632&pid=8135   Murat Yucel

7. *Marijuana & the Cancer Link -*

While this topic is hotly debated, this recent article is very concerning:

<u>Why cannabis is a greater cancer risk than tobacco</u>

by JENNY HOPE, Daily Mail 25/1/2017

Smoking cannabis is more harmful than cigarettes and more likely to trigger cancer, according to a report.

Just three cannabis 'joints' a day can cause the same amount of damage to the lungs as an entire packet of 20 cigarettes.

The British Lung Foundation says that when cannabis and tobacco are smoked together, the harmful effects are significantly worse.

Its research suggests young cannabis smokers may also be at greater risk of throat and gullet cancers.

The foundation found that tar from cannabis joints contains 50 per cent more cancer-causing toxins than cigarettes made from tobacco alone.

Dame Helena Shovelton, chief executive of the British Lung Foundation, said "The harmful effects of cannabis had been swept under the carpet."

"People are under the illusion it is safe to smoke cannabis. Our report shows it is very dangerous to lung health, at least as dangerous as tobacco."[14]

~~~~~~~~~~

As if all of this is not enough to make us stop and think, just recently I was having a private chat on Facebook with an old school friend of one of my sons. He had been battling drug addiction for some time. I was trying to offer some help as he told me the following :

His girlfriend had overdosed on heroin two years previously. He is virtually unemployable, despite several qualifications, because of drug related convictions. (Which he feels very wronged about).

According to this young man, all of his friends are either in prison, in psychiatric wards or dead because of drug use.

Over the past three or so years I had bumped into this young man a few times at the local shopping centre and as he had jokingly bragged about his drug use, I had tried to warn him about the possible dangers he was facing. What's more, I remember him as a young man with a good mind and high hopes for the future. I am so saddened by this, but this is the reality of drug addiction. I must add that of course for anyone battling addiction, there is always hope. As I have connected with this young man, I have seen a little of the cloud

---

[14] http://www.dailymail.co.uk/news/article-146853/Why-cannabis-greater-cancer-risk-tobacco.html   by Jenny Hope - Daily Mail July 25, 2017

that hangs over him, begin to lift. However, recovery from severe addiction can be quite a process.

From where I sit now, looking back over my life I can see so clearly just how crazy my behaviour was, but when you are in the middle of it all, using drugs, you simply can't see what's going on around you. You get so caught up in the drug scene that you are blinded to the reality of how it is changing you and affecting your behaviour, your attitudes and your relationships. Not to mention the damage to your health and your future career prospects.

I so wish I had taken another path. I wish that I had been on the other side of the law and chosen a career to do something so much more rewarding like becoming a police officer or even a paramedic. As a horse rider, my dream when I was younger was to join the mounted police force. As it turned out I missed out on countless career possibilities because of my later severe drug related health issues; regret I will carry forever.

What actually happens when you cross over into the dark world of drug taking is that you lose touch with reality and the drug world becomes your new reality. The unthinkable risks that you begin to take on a regular basis simply become 'normal' and it's not until you get out of that scene (if you do), that you can look back and see just how crazy that really was and how close you may have come to ending up dead or scarred for life. In the middle of living a drug and alcohol fuelled life, very few people stop to think about their future and how this behaviour might impact that. Living for the moment and thinking about where your next hit or smoke is coming from is usually all that matters to an addict.

Young people rarely consider 'future pain'.

5
Think First

"An unexpected journey"

As I touch on the topic of risk taking I am reminded of a few other frightening incidents that took place a couple of years before I moved to Pine Bay but visited regularly. It was also before either Vicki or I had a driver's licence.

On this particular day Vicki and I had walked to the shops from her family's property which was just outside of town, to hang out with some of the locals for a while, but we stayed longer than planned as we were supposed to be back for dinner by a particular time. As we headed home along the footpath aware that we had to make haste, a Kombi van slowed to a stop and a guy inside called out "Hey girls, do you want a lift?" Feeling very unsure about this I said, "No." but Vicki, knowing her mum would not be happy about our late return, said, "Yes. This will save us time." Still feeling uneasy I debated with her for a bit but finally saw her side and agreed to take up the offer.

The side door of the Kombi slid open with a loud groan as two other guys appeared in the back and welcomed us in. Bang! The door was shut as we suddenly realised that not only were we in an unknown van with three strangers, but there were two full size beer kegs in the back with them. The van took off. I don't remember much of the conversation, if any, but as we approached Vicki's home, she said, "Just here will do, thanks." We were a few blocks short of her place and the idea was to stop here so her parents wouldn't see us getting out of a stranger's van. The driver continued on as if he hadn't heard her. Vicki repeated her request but still there was no sign of slowing down.

By this time we had sailed right past her home and were speeding out on a long country road toward the cape with three men we didn't know. By now I had begun to freeze up as the gravity of the situation was sinking in and silently, desperately, I began to will the driver to stop. Vicki, becoming anxious, began to scream at him, which only enraged him as he planted his foot further down on the accelerator. She then grabbed him around the throat as fear filled us both and we began to realise what our fate might be. It was then that one of the other guys spoke up saying, "Hey mate, that's enough, I think you'd better let them out." Our now angry and possibly drunk driver ignored his call as my heart pounded inside my chest. Eventually, the third guy joined in and between the two of them they finally managed to convince the driver to stop. The van screeched to a halt as the door slid open once again and Vicki and I leapt out and headed quickly back toward home. We had been driven some way in the other direction past her home and now had a far longer walk as we hurried back toward the township.

I don't think I've mentioned the events of that afternoon to many people over the years but still today I can feel the immense sense of relief at being released from that van. Just a short time after that incident, a young girl we had met a few times at Pine Bay, was brutally raped and murdered and her body mercilessly dumped on Brighton Beach back in Melbourne. We had been with her and a group of friends earlier that very day! This incident shook us to the core. Whenever I recall memories of that time in the Kombi and think of the number of rapes and murders and missing persons that occur in our country, I shudder at the thought of what the outcome may have been if the other two guys had not spoken up.

There was only one other time that I hitched a ride with a stranger and that was pretty weird too. There was a surf carnival on at a beach about ten kilometres from Pine Bay and two other girls and I got a lift with a friend to the beach, but at the end of the day we had no lift home so we decided to hitch. A much older guy in a hot looking burnt orange Chrysler Charger pulled over and invited us to get in. We just wanted to get home so without much thought about the situation, we hopped in. The ride back to Pine Bay was so uncomfortable as the driver sped along, showing off his car and his driving skills and at the same time, began to make extremely sleazy and inappropriate comments to us. I was sitting in the front passenger seat and was so glad I wasn't alone. Being much younger than him and pretty much at his mercy, we didn't know how to respond to this weirdo and his sick comments and as we reached our destination, we leapt out of his car and quickly headed off without looking back.

These two stories have been included to remind anyone reading this account, of the shocking and potentially dangerous situations young and naïve people in particular, can put themselves in. It is in this time period, (usually between the ages of 12-25+) which is before the brain is fully mature, that we tend to think that we are indestructible, but of course nothing could be further from the truth. Many teens and young adults suffer harm or even death as a result of unnecessary risk taking. My hope is that by including each of my recollections, young readers in particular, will become more aware and thoughtful about situations they find themselves in.

Simply put… ' If in doubt, don't!'

6

Hallucinogens

"At the laundromat of space and time"

So here I was a few years on living the 'hippie' life in Pine Bay; working during the day (quite often stoned) and by night and on the weekends smoking and drinking without a care in the world and for that matter without a plan for the future. I had dropped my guard, and before long other drugs began to enter my world. I had heard a lot of talk about hallucinogenic substances like LSD, acid and 'magic' mushrooms (psilocybin mushrooms) but hadn't yet headed in that direction.

The first time I ever used a hallucinogenic substance was not actually what I had planned and in retrospect I can see that this led to a very dangerous situation.

I had driven with two girlfriends to a party in a small nearby town. It was a laid back sort of gathering and during the night several joints were passed around. Naturally being dope smokers, we all accepted their offer and joined in. However, unbeknown to us, these seemingly innocent little joints did not only contain marijuana. Someone had laced them with what I assume was dried 'magic' mushrooms and it wasn't until we were on our way home that the full impact of smoking these joints really hit all three of us.

Magic mushrooms have a powerful mind altering, hallucinogenic effect as the chemical they contain, psilocybin, is quickly converted by the body to psilocin. Once ingested and metabolized it then acts on the serotonin receptors in the brain. The mind-altering effects of psilocybin typically lasts for two to six hours, although for individuals under the influence of psilocybin the effects may seem to last much longer since the drug can distort the perception of time. A common nick-name for this feeling is 'tripping'.

The road we had to take to return home was rather narrow and bumpy and at one point had a very sharp hairpin bend. I don't remember actually leaving the party, but I certainly do remember the journey home. Magic mushrooms have a powerful hallucinogenic effect and as this was an effect none of us was expecting, especially combined with the marijuana, the drive home became pretty frightening. I was having a lot trouble focusing on the road as my sight and perception had been severely distorted by the chemicals swirling around in my brain. This meant that I had to concentrate extremely hard to stay on the correct side of that dark, winding country road.

At one point Megan, who was sitting in the back, began to freak out, urging me to stop as she called out,

"Pull over! Pull over! There's someone behind us flashing their headlights at us." (I think she though it was the cops.) I looked into the rear-view mirror and saw the 'flashing' lights and pulled over into the gravel on the side of the road. The car travelling behind just flew past us and it was then that we realised the lights had only appeared to be flashing as the car had been bouncing along the bumpy road. Phew!

I slowly took off again to continue our journey home, until I started to experience another delusion. It began to occur to me that I hadn't noticed the hairpin bend that I knew was coming up, and this thought took my head to another place. I started to believe that I had actually missed the bend and with the intensity of the bumps, greatly magnified by the hallucinations I was having, I thought I was speeding through a paddock and toward the cliff edge that I knew was at the other end of this paddock. Then, just as suddenly, the sharp bend appeared before us and I snapped back into the reality of the situation. Somehow, we made it home that night and later, being young and stupid, and of course having survived, we laughed at the memory of that incident.

What had happened to us that night was an experience that should never have taken place. The practice of spiking drinks or joints or bongs etc. with substances other than what the user is expecting, is a very dangerous and all too common occurrence. We could well have been killed on that night. Driving in that state of mind, where I could barely see the road, could easily have led to disaster and we might have become just another three of the State of Victoria's road toll statistics.

Tragically in this country, we lose way too many young people on our roads, because of driving under the influence of drugs or alcohol. Reader, please take note.

Despite this frightening incident, a little while later when we'd almost forgotten just how bad that night had been, we learned that 'magic mushrooms' grew in abundance not far from our little home. We were blindly sliding down that slippery slope and without a thought of any possible consequences a few friends and I decided to give them a go. We figured that without being mixed with weed, the experience wouldn't be so bad. So we knowingly took our first magic mushrooms.

It was a wild, stormy afternoon and the euphoria and distorted perception I felt from having ingested the mushrooms was like nothing I had ever experienced. Time stood still and I began to feel like I never wanted to return to reality and we drove around for some time and then wandered through the 'enchanted forest' looking to pick more.

You see this is the lure of all drugs; they so often start by giving you an amazing experience, but from my experience and that of most other drug users I have ever known, this is the trap. The more you use of any particular drug, the less fun it becomes and for us it wasn't that long before the 'trips' began to turn bad. I saw several friends having a 'bad trip' and totally flipping out as paranoia took over. I had my share of terrifying moments too.

Then there are those who I now consider the 'lucky ones'. These are the people who have a really frightening experience the first time they ever take an illicit drug. One freaky incident can prevent them from ever using drugs again and as a consequence their lives are not destroyed by this lifestyle. I so wish I'd been one of them.

But the thing is we had assumed that the bad experience was only brought on by the fact that we had (unknowingly) taken two drugs together. Young people using drugs think they are such experts. Really we had no idea of what we were getting into.

There was one other incident that occurred, after yet another night of ingesting the mushrooms, where both Meg and I woke up with weird physical side-effects. My thumbs weren't working properly. It was as if they had no bones in them and Megs legs kept collapsing on her. We had taken so many of these potent little fungi that I think we were beginning to poison ourselves. This was something we had never even considered. So we had a break from using them for a while. But that wasn't the end of it. We had become totally blind to the level of risks we were taking and by this time we were in way too deep and before long this behaviour resumed.

~~~~~~~~~~

One night things really turned bad for both Meg and me. We'd had a few friends around and all of us had smoked dope and eaten 'mushies'. (By this time we had thrown caution to the wind and we were regularly mixing marijuana with any other substance we used.)

After our friends left to go home both Meg and I went to bed; the doors to our rooms were at right angles to each other. It was late and I lay in bed trying to sleep but was not having any success as the drugs in my system were keeping me awake. All of a sudden my door began to open. The silvery moonlight streaming through my window gave me a clear view. Staring straight at me was a tall, terrifying half man, half dog with bright yellow eyes; I guess you would call it some sort of werewolf. I was absolutely frozen with fear. I held the sheets up to my face and my breathing stopped. It seemed like it was there forever but then it moved back, pulling my door shut with it. I breathed again. About thirty seconds passed and the house was suddenly filled with blood curdling screams from the room next door. 'It' had gone into Meg's room.

Fear filled every inch of my being. I had two choices. The first was to head for the front door and run for my life, but that could be disastrous, we were in the bush and it was night time; there was nowhere to run. My second option was to run into Meg's room and help her to fight off this freaky, grotesque creature. I opted for the second choice. I raced into the room next door only to find that not only had Meg also seen this terrifying creature, but she was now having another completely different experience. Meg was hysterical, convinced that someone was being stabbed to death in our front yard. I heard nothing. We eventually managed to calm each other down and went back to bed.

I don't know what that was about but there was no doubt, the potent chemicals we had ingested had absolutely messed with our heads creating a terrifying experience that will stay with us forever.

Despite this ordeal, a short time later the partying continued.

**Note: It is illegal to use magic mushrooms in Australia and police regularly patrol areas where they grow.

~~~~~~~~~

Recently, just as I began to touch on the topic of hallucinogenic substances, a tragic story hit the news about the son of a well-known Australian rock musician, Nick Cave, lead singer of 'Nick Cave and the Bad Seeds'. Cave and his family moved to Brighton, England some years ago and earlier this year Nick's fifteen year old son, Arthur, (who also had a twin brother) had fallen to his death from a steep cliff. (July 14 2015)

The news report on the findings from the inquest into his shocking death stated that Arthur and a friend had taken LSD (a hallucinogen) after first researching the drug on line. These sites give information about the duration of the experience etc., but little information is given about any possible negative effects or the darker side to LSD.

The area they chose to take the LSD (trip or acid) was at the site of Rottingdean Windmill, on the south coast of England near Brighton where they lived. There was a huge expanse of grass, a road and a simple wire fence between the boys and the cliff face; so I assume the boys felt quite safe.

The report went on to quote Arthur's friend who said, "The night all started well and we were in 'good spirits and happy' ".... But apparently things soon began to turn bad as the potent chemicals the boys had ingested began to cause vivid hallucinations and instil fear. Panic set in and the pair separated and lost sight of each other. It was reported that Arthur sent a text message to a friend that read, "Where am I, Where am I?" A woman driving slowly along the seafront with her daughter saw Arthur looking disoriented and "stumbling along a patch of grass close to the cliff edge." She pulled her car over and got out to help. But it was too late. By the time she reached the area where she had seen him, Arthur had disappeared over the edge of the sheer cliff. A man cycling home from work also witnessed the fall. The much loved teen died shortly after in hospital with the hospital statement concluding "he had suffered multiple traumatic injuries leading to death after ingesting LSD."

Tragically, this is a devastating reality of the potential outcome of using hallucinogenic drugs.

Arthur's family's touching comment about their son stated, "He was a bright, shiny, funny, complex boy and we loved him dearly." *Source - The Guardian & ABC News* [15]

As a former drug user and as a mother my heart really goes out to the Cave family…. Today I realise it could so easily have been my parents having to deal with the loss of their much-loved and only daughter.

Sadly, this is not the only incident where a person taking LSD or other hallucinogenic drugs, has come to grief and it will probably not be the last. There have been numerous reports around the world of LSD and other hallucinogenic drug use leading to accidental death.

In 2013 a Year 12 school student, from Perth in Western Australia, tragically died after falling from a balcony at a Hotel in Scarborough. He was only sixteen years old and he had been with friends celebrating his school ball when he had taken synthetic LSD. The report stated that after consuming the drug the teen thought that he could fly and fell to his death. This is an example of the powerful mind distorting effect psychedelic drugs can have on anyone using them.

The drug had been purchased by a friend from the online website called Silk Road. After his son's death, the young man's devastated father campaigned

---

[15] http://www.dailymail.co.uk/news/article-3311680/Musician-Nick-Cave-wife-arrive-inquest-death-son-Arthur-15-died-falling-cliff.html - Martin Robinson -Mailonline & Mario Ledwith Daily Mail - Nov 10, 2015

tirelessly to have the site closed down and in October 2013 he was said to be "over the moon" following the news that the website had been shut down and the mastermind behind it arrested.

" *'The website mastermind' was jailed for life for his role in creating and running the multi-million-dollar business used as a black market for drugs.*"[16]

While this is great news, the same technology is still available and copycat sites do exist. Of course the Australian Federal Police are well aware of this and these sites operate at a high risk of being detected.

Over the years, the range of illicit drugs available has continued to vary and grow, although many of the original illicit or so called 'recreational' substances, such as marijuana, heroin, cocaine speed and LSD which have been around for decades (or in some cases, centuries), are still heavily infiltrating our society. Combined with these, today we have moved well and truly into the age of synthetic drugs. Just about any drug on the market can be synthesised and in order to keep these drugs off the 'illicit' drug list, the chemical composition of each particular substance is regularly 'tweaked' to stay ahead of the law. Illicit drug production and distribution is 'big money' to the law-breakers involved! I'll touch on this aspect again later.

---

[16] http://www.abc.net.au/news/2015-05-30/father-blames-silk-road-creator-for-sons-drug-death/6509262   by Laura Gartry - ABC News - May 31, 2015

This also means users have no idea of exactly what is in the substance they are taking and subsequently no idea of how their body will react to the chemicals used.

(Note: even if a person does know exactly what is contained in the drugs they are about to use, there is no guarantee that they will not have a bad or even severe reaction to that substance, in the same way that some are allergic to penicillin and some are not. An example is Ecstasy. When a person has a severe reaction to MDMA (ecstasy) the purity and quantity is insignificant. The reaction is what it is – severe; even deadly.

*** New laws have been rolled out across Victoria and other states and countries regarding synthetic drugs. See Chapter 23 for more on this.

7

Wild Days

"as all hell……..with brakes loose"

    I was never going to use what I considered to be 'hard' drugs, but one day a friend came to visit and told me that he'd been using heroin. I was pretty shocked at first but also curious. I knew this friend had a full-time office job and besides he didn't look all that unhealthy. This was certainly not the image I had pictured of a heroin user. Any portrayal I had seen or imagined of a 'junkie' was one of a sickly, bedraggled, shadow of a human being whose life consisted of living on the streets, entrenched in crime in order to raise enough funds to support a drug habit (which sadly, is the case for some).

    So, with this normal-looking person standing before me, I decided these images must have been wrong and besides I was curious, so I asked if he could get some for me. I just wanted to try it, to see what all the hype was about. I was strong. This wouldn't get me. And of course, I would then be able to say "Yeah, I've used heroin," how 'cool' would that sound? The lies, the deception; my guard was by now fully down and we lined up a day and I had my first taste of heroin.

Like I said, I was only ever going to try this once, to experience it and discover what all the hype was about. But this is a very addictive drug and before long I had my second 'taste' and then my third as heroin gradually began to creep into my life, and so the downward spiral continued.

After three years of living in that beautiful little coastal town, I decided to move back to Melbourne. I had by now had some relationship issues and just needed to get away from that place and the memories it held. I was no longer the innocent young girl who had first moved out of my family home, but like all of us, deep down I had an ache in my heart to find fulfilment and meaning in my life.

Not long after moving back to Melbourne I met a guy named David. He was warm and intelligent with a witty sense of humour and he introduced me to a cultural side of Melbourne I had not known; one vastly different to the country lifestyle I had been living over the past few years, and before long we began a relationship. It just so happened, that David had been using heroin for a few years. The thing is, when you associate with friends who use drugs, it's quite natural to meet other people who are also drug users… So, now

I had the contacts in Melbourne and gradually my heroin use increased.

I began an office job in South Melbourne with a large company that imported musical instruments and before long I moved in with David. Our lives had become a world of work, drugs, alcohol and parties. As well as heroin, or smack as we called it, we often used speed, a drug which kept us awake for hours or even days at a time and took a terrible toll on our bodies. (I am so thankful that although Ice (Methamphetamine) has been around since the 1960's, it wasn't so widely available back then; I'll get to that topic later)

David also joined the company I was working for in South Melbourne and as it was very close to the suburb where we scored our drugs, we often called in on the way home and did just that. Even worse, many times we slipped out at lunch time, scored heroin and either hit up in a local park, or we'd go back to work to have it. David would have his hit in the toilets downstairs and then buzz me on the intercom, I would then go down and collect my share (which he had mixed in a syringe for me) and I would take it to the toilets near my desk and have my hit. I'm not sure if anyone ever caught on. Possibly not, as this was a company with a culture of long lunches with excessive alcohol consumption. When I think of it now it makes me shudder to imagine what would have happened if one of us had overdosed in the toilet cubicle at work.

To a person who has had nothing to do with drugs, this behaviour might seem unbelievable, but believe me, for anyone who is involved in drugs this is just the way it is. The more that you use, the more you begin to slide down into that dark hole without really being able to see how far you have fallen.

~~~~~~~~~

As I recall all of these memories, I just want to pause to say... I am not proud of any of this. I'm just telling the story, as it was, in the hope that anyone reading might come to recognise the pain, suffering and hopelessness that drug use brings. If I could turn back the clock and change any of this to erase the heartache and pain this later brought to me and my family, I would do so in a heartbeat. As I indicated previously, I was brought up in a loving, supportive family and was really quite a shy and very straight young girl, all through my teenage years. But I made one huge mistake and opened the door into the dangerous world of drugs. Once this door had been opened, I entered into a bizarre, abnormal world that eventually just became normal for me. Even though I knew that this behaviour was illegal, my judgement had become blurred and the lie of 'this is ok' became as truth.

~~~~~~~~~

The downward spiral I had now found myself caught up in, was so well and truly in motion that the following events didn't even seem that shocking to me.

I had slipped down that slope to the point where I was totally blinded to the dangers of this lifestyle.

The reality is, as we all know people using hard drugs can overdose! It was not uncommon for me to be sitting in a group of drug users, in particular heroin, (although many other drugs can also lead to overdose and death), when suddenly someone would stop breathing and begin to turn blue. Another person would jump to their rescue and give them mouth-to-mouth resuscitation and they would soon start breathing again. Although it was a bit frightening to witness, because of the quick recovery, it didn't look that serious to me. I never saw anyone using proper CPR (Cardio Pulmonary Resuscitation). We did not know what we were doing. We were playing with fire!

The following story is one that took place over thirty years ago and yet it was so terrifying that I can remember every detail as if it were yesterday.

8

Terror

"Not the whisper of a sound"

One of the most terrifying nights of my life began with a fun night out at the Crystal Ballroom in Fitzroy Street, St. Kilda. 'The Models'[17] were playing and they were pretty big at the time. David and I and a few other friends joined a huge crowd in a packed, smoke-filled room and drank and danced the night away. At one point David said that he was going to the toilet and disappeared from sight. I was having too much fun to notice how long he had been missing and at the end of the night he was back with me and we headed home. I can still remember laughing and staggering arm in arm

---

[17] *In 2010, tragically, one of the founding members of the Models took his own life. This particular band member had had a well-known long-term battle with drug and alcohol addiction. While I don't know the exact circumstances behind his decision to take his life, what I do know is that very sadly, drugs and alcohol are often linked to depression and suicide.*

with a few friends down the street to our car. I had no idea of the nightmare that lay ahead ...

We were living at Black Rock at this stage and we somehow made it home. By now I had the munchies and decided to cook up some muffins with egg, bacon, tomato and cheese and set about doing that. David said that he was feeling hot and sweaty from the over-crowded room we had been in and decided to have a shower. I merrily cooked away and when the food was finally ready I knocked on the bathroom door to let him know. There was no response, so I opened the door to stick my head in and call out a bit louder. The room was filled with steam. All David had managed to do was to turn on the hot tap. (What I didn't know was that while he had disappeared from the venue to 'go to the toilet' he had actually slipped out of the venue and scored heroin.) This is a really dangerous mix. Heroin on its own can kill. Even alcohol alone can kill. But when you mix any two or more chemical substances together or in fact any drug with alcohol, you are really putting your body under immense strain and greatly increasing the risk of overdose. The human body is not built to withstand this kind of assault.

I looked across through the thick mist of steam and there was David, naked and slumped over an old disused oil heater. He had overdosed! I freaked. I raced into the bathroom and pulled his limp body onto the floor. He was colourless and his head hit the floor with a thud. I fell to my knees beside him to begin mouth-to-mouth resuscitation, but his jaw was clamped so tightly shut that I had to use all the strength I could summon to force his mouth open. I was in an utter panic. I had seen plenty of ODs, but I had never seen anyone looking so far gone … so dead.

I began to blow madly, furiously into his mouth over and over and over again. Nothing was happening. I continued on in a state of absolute terror for at least fifteen to twenty minutes.   Utterly exhausted and with no response from him at all, I stood up realising that it was no use. He was gone. Here I was in the middle of the night by myself, with my dead boyfriend. What now? I could hardly breathe from the terror and the effort I had exerted trying to bring him back to life. Who do I call? An ambulance? There would be police! How could I tell his mother? I was crying, screaming, begging David to breathe.

My head was spinning and in a state of excruciating fear I fell back to my knees and desperately continued to blow air into his lungs with every ounce of strength I could muster. Finally, after at least another fifteen or twenty minutes, an eerie groan came from David's mouth. I breathed some more air into his mouth then shook him, slapped him and shook him again.

At last, he began to regain consciousness.

Throughout the remainder of that night, every time David closed his eyes, I prodded him to make sure he stayed alive. I could not believe what had happened to us and just how close it had been. The memory of that night will stay with me forever.

For the next three days I could barely breathe, I had blown so hard and for so long in my effort to resuscitate David that my entire throat and windpipe area was red raw. You would think an ordeal like that would be enough to turn us off drugs forever. Unfortunately not! As for David, well, he'd been unconscious the whole time and really didn't comprehend the severity of the O.D. I think he just thought he was so tough! And with him still using, how could I stop? It was so addictive. It's just not that easy.

~~~~~~~~~

I was not immune to drug overdoses either. I actually overdosed on heroin three times. Twice resuscitated by David and once incredibly waking from a drug and alcohol overdose that left me unconscious on the floor for nearly three hours.

One of these incidents stands out in particular because of the reaction of a guy named Tony, who was with us at the time. We were in a flat in St. Kilda where we had divided up some smack (heroin) and we'd all had our 'hit'. Afterwards, I lit a cigarette and accidentally dropped the box of matches on the floor. I leaned down to pick them up and didn't come back up again. I had overdosed and was slipping into unconsciousness.

Of course I remember nothing of the next few minutes, but suddenly I found myself lying on the floor with a wet face, and Tony was jumping up and down almost crying at the sight of me regaining consciousness. He had been terrified at the sight of me unconscious as David battled to get me breathing again. Apparently I had been 'gone' for a while and David had given me mouth-to-mouth resuscitation while Tony poured a glass of water over my face in an attempt to revive me.

We really were playing with fire! But still we were blinded to the possibility of this ever actually taking our lives. No one ever thinks it will happen to them! It only happens to other people! What's more, I always had an excuse as to why I had overdosed. I was tired or I hadn't been feeling well. How about …**I was using a deadly drug!** That's why I overdosed!!

Unfortunately, we knew of friends who did succumb to drugs and it was always a massive shock to learn of their death; something that took some time to get our head around. Another young life tragically wasted and yet as I keep stressing, most people who use drugs, still believe that it will never happen to them.

It may seem that drug overdoses are not that big a deal as I have listed cases where others have managed to successfully resuscitate victims. However, nothing could be further from the truth, as many users OD alone or in a group of people who are also drug-affected and as a result, are unable to recognize that a person is in danger. The following scenario relates to one such tragic course of events.

A popular young man, whom I had met on one occasion, had been to a party with a group of friends where they had all used heroin. (This could just as easily have been GHB, Ecstasy, Ice or Ketamine etc.) Later the group headed home in a car and on their arrival went inside. As they had all been affected by the drugs, they didn't notice that their friend was still in the car … and he was in a bad way. The following morning, to the shock, horror and disbelief of his friends, the young man was found dead in the back seat of the car, leaving yet another grief-stricken family to pick up the pieces. The problem was that the group of friends had been too 'out of it' to notice that their friend had overdosed, which in turn meant that any possible chance of resuscitation was missed. Tragically, this happens all too often.

Another dangerous practice is where people use drugs while they are alone and have no one to help if they are in trouble. As Heroin is a depressant drug, it slows down the messages between the brain and the body. Once a person begins to overdose, they 'nod off' and slip from sleep to unconsciousness and their breathing stops, followed by their heart and brain shutting down resulting in death. Without assistance they simply cannot bring themselves back to life.

~~~~~~~~~~

It may appear that this all happened long ago and that not much is reported about heroin ODs these days. Make no mistake, heroin is still around and, I guess, could be called the silent killer. Some years ago, long after my illness, my dad employed a man for a few weeks to re-paint the interior of his city business. He was a handsome, fit looking young man with his whole life ahead of him. One day he asked my dad if he could have his wages a few days early as he was having a 'dinner party' and needed the money for food. Well, food was not the only thing on the shopping list! (If in fact there was a dinner party at all. Drug users concoct any number of 'stories' to obtain money to score their drugs. I know we did). That night his girlfriend died of a heroin overdose. As if that was not tragic enough, about eight months later we learnt of this young man's death, also from a drug overdose. Among the many death notices, there was one tragically sad notice in the obituaries from his adoring, grieving grandfather who was trying to come to terms with the pointless loss of his beloved grandson.

~~~~~~~~~~

Between finishing Year 12 and the start of his apprenticeship, our elder son had a holiday job with a young panel beater. He was a likeable young man in his twenties and a few years back we learned of his death; once again from a heroin overdose. I really grieved over the next few days as I pictured his smiling face and easy-going manner and recalled that he had only recently been married and had a young baby. In fact, this deeply affected me. As one who had used drugs and understood addiction, I knew that he had most likely not expected to die and over the following few days this really began to mess with my head; my mind flooded with a frightening image of this young man slipping from life to death, screaming "No, no, I didn't mean this to happen." I'm sure he thought he would just get stoned again as usual and go on and use drugs again another day. Once again I stress, everyone thinks it will never happen to them. It's always somebody else! To make things even worse, this young man was an only child. His parents had lost their precious only child to one of the most pointless deaths possible; a drug overdose.

~ ~ ~ ~ ~ ~ ~ ~ ~

And then there is another side of drug use. Illicit drugs are expensive and users will stoop to all kinds of extreme lows in their desperation to find money to buy drugs to feed their addiction.

One day, out of the blue, David and I had a visit from three guys who we knew but were not close to; they had come with some smack (heroin) to sell to us. Naturally, we took up the offer. They came in and we all sat around and indulged together. They stayed for an hour or so. After they left David and I both commented that they had seemed to be looking around, 'casing' the place while they were there and sure enough about a month later it happened. We came home from work one day and found the front door wide open. My dog Mandu, who should have been in the back yard, was sitting on the front porch wagging her tail and 'smiling'. So much for our watch dog! I felt sick in the stomach as I realised what had happened. While we had been at work, our home had been broken into and both our T.V. and Hi Fi system (and a few other possessions) were stolen. We reported it to the police, but naturally could not inform them of our suspicions as that would also implicate us. We knew who the culprits were.

About six months later, I had a call from the local police informing me that officers in a police helicopter had spotted three young men breaking into another home in the area. The three were caught, arrested and taken to the local police station where they were questioned. They admitted to committing thirteen house burglaries including the one at our home. I asked the officer if he could tell me the names of the offenders and he obliged. Sure enough, they were the same so-called 'friends' who had visited us and 'cased' our home a few months earlier. Of course, I could not say that I knew any of these guys as once again this would implicate us. The sad truth is that when drugs are involved, people get desperate and friendship lines can be crossed without a second thought.

The crazy thing is all of these events took place while we were both working full-time and attending social and family functions etc. To anyone who didn't know any different David and I were just a normal everyday couple. We were functioning addicts.

My life had slipped so far down this hole; I couldn't see what was right before me.

9
Repercussions

"Like a piece of junk mail, shoved under deaths' door"

Our life continued on with work, drugs, alcohol and parties until one night, while we were dining out at a pancake restaurant in the city (Melbourne), I suddenly became extremely itchy all over my body. I had to go into the ladies' room to strip off and scratch frantically. We headed home and the following morning I woke up with red welts all over my body. I drove down to the local Sandringham Hospital where I was diagnosed with some sort of allergic reaction. I was given some antihistamines and sent home. Three days later the welts disappeared but I woke up feeling stiff in every joint of my body. This turned into a severe form of arthritis so my GP referred me to a rheumatologist who did a blood test which revealed Hepatitis B. This very debilitating and painful arthritis lasted for three and a half months.

Then the Hepatitis B symptoms followed. Hepatitis B is a serious illness on its own, but as I was later to discover, I also had complications. Although I had no jaundice, which I probably should have had, I was very lethargic and lost a lot of weight. I was given two months off work. At the end of that two months I was no better, so I was given a further two months off. Still the symptoms did not abate and I was given yet another two months off work. Unbeknown to me or to my doctor something else was going on inside of me.

Because of my sickness I moved from the house that David and I shared to my parents' home. By this time I was fed up with being sick so when I heard of a party in Black Rock, I decided to take some analgesics and go out and try to enjoy myself. It was a bikie party and there was an abundance of alcohol and speed (amphetamine) so, feeling a bit better because of the analgesics I had taken, I decided a little speed wouldn't do any harm and I snorted a small line.

When using speed you tend to lose track of time. I'm not sure exactly when it was, but while I was in the backyard, suddenly a violent fight broke out between two girls. It was wild; biting, scratching, hitting, hair pulling and kicking not to mention the language. A few people went to step in, but others said, "Just let them get it out of their system," and the fight continued. After that, with all the drugs and tension in the air, just as suddenly I witnessed another guy getting 'king hit' (now known as a coward punch or one punch) and as he hit the ground, a whole group of other guys laid into him. In my altered state of mind it was kind of surreal. I was watching it in silhouette as there was a bright spotlight behind them, and I remember thinking, "What a pack of cowards taking on one man like that."

I guess it was a couple of hours later when the host of the party (who had been the coward puncher) came up to me and asked "How is David?" I didn't understand until he explained that it was David who had been bashed. I demanded he look for him. I found David's sister and after frantically searching for a while, we headed home. David was there. He had staggered home and was trying to drum up some friends to go back with him for a pay back. The room was filled with tension as his sister and I tried to calm him down. Suddenly, the back of my neck became stiff and I felt an agonising pain like the stab of a knife, and that was the last thing I remember ...

Three days later I woke up in the Alfred Hospital, Melbourne. I'd had a series of Grand Mal seizures (convulsions) and David had tried to resuscitate me while his sister had called an ambulance. I was rushed straight to the hospital. (In writing this I just had a really weird image of what that scene must have been like, as I had been convulsing uncontrollably in an ambulance ride I have absolutely no recollection of; a freaky thought.)

Over the following few days I drifted in and out of consciousness as the seizures continued. My condition was assessed as a drug and alcohol overdose, although I had definitely had no alcohol and only a very small line of speed. The assumption of alcohol came because David had been drinking and he had given me mouth-to-mouth resuscitation, leaving the smell of alcohol on my breath. I was sent back home again, but the doctors were totally unaware of what was really going on in my body.

Over the next couple of weeks I became weaker and weaker. By this time the average Hepatitis B patient should have been improving. Mum took me to a new doctor who did an ECG (electro-cardiogram) on my heart. He was shocked by the result and immediately referred me for an urgent appointment to see a specialist, a Professor in haematology at the Alfred Hospital Melbourne; I was to see him the following day. By this time even the least amount of physical effort left me exhausted and breathless. Mum drove me to the hospital and dropped me at the entrance, where I collapsed on the steps while she parked the car. The specialist (Professor Firkin), whose clinic I was about to attend, happened to walk by. On seeing the state I was in, he promptly ordered a wheel-chair to carry me to his consulting room.

I was quickly assessed and diagnosed with acute heart and kidney failure. Professor Firkin immediately called for a hospital gurney. I collapsed onto the bed and was raced through the hospital corridors to the Cardiac Care Unit (CCU) (Intensive care heart ward).

At that point I was given less than two hours to live! In fact my family was informed that I could die "at any moment!"

A code blue alert rang throughout the hospital as the emergency doctors who were on call raced to my side. I was attended to and examined by the Alfred Hospital's top heart, kidney and immunology specialists who diagnosed me with a form of cardiomyopathy. They said that my only chance of survival would be to have a heart transplant, but I would need it within the next two hours. Of course, it would be impossible to find a matching heart and set up surgery for such a complex operation in just a few hours. But there was also another problem. My renal failure was so severe that my kidneys would not withstand the surgery. I had less than five percent function in both kidneys.

In his attempt to break the shocking news to my mother, Professor Firkin said, "Kerryn is in an extremely serious condition. We do not expect her to live!" He paused and then added, "We cannot hold out any hope, this condition has a 99.9% mortality rate." My family quickly gathered around as I lay in the Cardiac Care Unit (CCU) waiting to die.

I felt like dying. My heart was so enlarged that it was racing at about 300-400 beats per minute rather than the normal 70-80 beats and because two major organs were shutting down, my body was filling up with fluid. As a result of this I had pulmonary oedema; my lungs were flooding and I could barely breathe. I ached all over, my blood pressure was sky high and I had huge lumps of fluid all over my body.

Because of the acute kidney failure, my fluid intake was severely restricted. I was deprived of the elixir of life...water...and I vividly recall begging for just an ice block or even a wet flannel to suck on, as thirst began to overwhelm me.

The room was filled with a myriad of monitors and machines. I had a blood pressure cuff on, an octopus drip pumping different drugs into my arm, a urine catheter connected and an oxygen mask strapped to my face. I clearly remember that time as I gasped for every breath. It was as though the air could not quite reach my lungs and I pulled the mask off and on again over and over desperately trying to ease the excruciating agony. It felt like I was drowning. I recall doctor after doctor lifting my hands to look for signs of haemorrhaging or septic shock in my fingers as they battled to keep me alive.

It was at this time that a brilliant young immunologist-rheumatologist (now Associate Professor), Peter Ryan, was on duty and he managed to diagnose my condition. It had now been labelled *'Polyarteritis Nodosa',* which translated means, 'many inflamed arteries and nodules'. This had apparently been caused by some malfunction of my auto-immune system. Rather than fight the Hepatitis B disease, my anti-bodies had attacked my body and as this was a rare condition it had not been picked up earlier.

(In 2010 it was reported that smoking marijuana can suppress the body's immune system. It would be interesting to know if there was a link between my heavy marijuana smoking and the auto-immune malfunction I suffered after contracting Hepatitis B)[18]

There I lay, my life rapidly slipping away as my stunned and devastated family hovered around. I had always managed to hide my drug problem from them and now, not only had they just been informed by the doctors that this was all drug related, but they were about to lose me. What had gone so wrong? Where was the healthy, happy young girl they once knew?

My doctors were amazing. They administered many different drugs including high doses of steroids and an immunosuppressive medication, called Cyclophosphamide, in an attempt to reverse the inflammation to my organs and arterial system (approval had to be given from Canberra, the capital city of Australia, before this drug could be used). However, by this time the damage to my body was so severe, that to turn things around in just a couple of hours was "out of the question" and this is just what my family was told. At the time, mum refused to let the doctors tell me that I was expected to die. She reasoned that not knowing might give me the strength to fight on.

---

[18] https://www.livescience.com/9008-marijuana-suppresses-immune-system.html
by Live Science Staff - November 29, 2010

I had no fight left in me at all. The only hope left for me would have to be a miracle. My family was told to pray.

Amazingly I survived that night and the next few days. However, on my fourth day in the CCU while still gravely ill, I was sent off to have an angiogram to assess the damage to my heart, kidneys and arterial system. The result was bad. The specialists informed my family that the damage to my body was so severe that "Nobody could possibly survive it." I remained in the Coronary Care Unit waiting to die.

On my seventh day in hospital, my doctors were scratching their heads, wondering why 'this young woman' was still alive. I was sent off to have another scan of my heart and the following day the results came through. I had three different specialists visit me and their words were, "This is amazing!", 'That is not the same heart", "It's like you have a new heart!" Incredibly, my heart was now beating strongly and had returned to normal size. However, both of my kidneys were still severely damaged and I remained in hospital for almost five months, while they very slowly improved.

And as you can gather, despite all of these dire prognoses, I rather miraculously survived and I am still here to tell the story. I was one very lucky girl.

10

What will it take?

"Lost in a weave of a wicked web"

My stay in hospital was long and depressing. I was so sick and unbelievably thin and weak. I can still remember the first time that I actually stood up for an entire shower, instead of sitting on a plastic chair. Halfway through I began to shake all over, but I was determined not to give in and sit down. I made it!

Apart from friends' visits and mum's daily visit, my older brother, who went to church, had told his minister, Brian, of my plight and although I'd had nothing to do with the church, Brian, who naturally had experience in counselling, visited regularly. This was actually great for my sanity as he helped me to 'unload' some of the stuff that was spinning in my mind. Lying around for so many months too weak for any physical activity really messed with my head. I was however, fortunate that I was blessed at birth with a positive outlook on life. Regardless, this was really putting my normally optimistic and determined personality to the test.

After about two and a half months in hospital I was allowed out for weekend leave. I went home and a friend came and picked me up and took me to her place for the afternoon. She and her partner were smoking some 'bongs' and I begged them to give me just a small cone. Foolishly, despite how delicate my health was, I still felt the desperate need to fit in! I guess I also didn't want others to think of me as 'the sickie'. They finally relented and I had a very small pipe. After a few hours I began to realise that I was far more stoned than I should have been and panic began to set in. Suddenly, it really hit me that I had just had heart and kidney failure and that mixing hash with the medication I was on was pretty stupid. I lay down for a while hoping to recover, but this made no difference. I was in a really bad state and I asked my friend to drive me home. By this time I was totally spinning out and now I had to face my parents. They quickly drove me back to the hospital. They were furious. No one spoke on that journey.

On my return to the ward my doctors ordered a blood test. They wanted to check just what drugs I had taken. They didn't believe me when I told them that it was only a small amount of hash/marijuana, and who could blame them? The next day my head specialist, Professor Firkin, came into my room with his tribe of student doctors and stood at the end of my bed. With his usual calm voice of authority he said, "Kerryn, God helps those who help themselves". He then spun around and marched out. I felt so small. That was the last time I ever used illicit drugs.

A female specialist, who was also supervising my case, was so angry with me that she refused to talk to me. I don't blame her at all for that. My case had put my doctors under immense pressure as they agonised over balancing drug doses and combinations, all the while trying not to destroy my ovaries, just in case. Once again mum stepped in. She pleaded with my doctor to forgive me, saying that I knew I had messed up and that I needed all the support I could get to make it through this. Following this latest episode, I also had to see three psychiatrists to prove that I was actually sane. My doctors had been really excited as they had just managed to get a brand new product – Interferon – in from Finland for me, at a cost of $80,000 to the Government. That was a lot of money in 1982. This product had never been used in Australia before. I was about to be their 'guinea pig'. Now they had to make sure that they were not going to waste it on someone who might just go out and continue to use illicit drugs and possibly overdose. Somehow I managed to pass the sanity test.

Interferon was used in an attempt to cure the Hepatitis B, as while I still carried the Hep B virus, my antibodies could at any time reignite the condition which could again become potentially lethal. Interferon was still in the experimental stage and consequently the dose

I was given was more than I could tolerate. This caused me to vomit a number of times, throwing up the medication that was keeping my blood pressure down. As a result my blood pressure rapidly increased and I began to have more Grand Mal seizures (convulsions). The seizures were so violent that I fell out of bed, ripping a drip out of my arm. This time I fell into a coma. Once again a code blue alert rang throughout the hospital as all of the emergency doctors raced to my side. I was gravely ill in the ICU and once more my family rallied around preparing for the worst. Again, incredibly, I pulled through; but only just. I had been unconscious for three days with no indication at all of whether I would ever wake up.

During my stay in hospital, I underwent many different tests including a lumbar puncture, a bone marrow test, an angiogram, hundreds of blood tests and scans and one of the more memorable ones, a kidney biopsy. I was told this particular test should take about thirty minutes. But there was a problem. Both of my kidneys had been so severely damaged that they were small, shrivelled and covered in tough scar tissue. According to the scans, they were both about the size and appearance of a walnut (healthy human kidneys are roughly the size of a fist). I was given a Valium drip to help me relax throughout the procedure so I didn't really notice the time that passed, although I do remember the doctor's anguish and frustration.

My kidney damage was so severe that the procedure took three and a half hours and they were still not able to penetrate the tissue enough to get a sample from either kidney. What I do remember vividly was that for the entire procedure I lay face down with my arms above my head. At the end of the three and a half hours, my arms were locked in that position and this led to a very slow, painful process, as I tried to lower them again. By this point my kidney function had reached approximately forty percent and that's where the improvement stopped.

After almost five long months of fighting for my life, I finally left the Alfred Hospital Melbourne, with a strong heart but only forty percent function in both of my now badly scarred kidneys.

~~~~~~~~~

On another note, a few years back (many years after this hospital stay) I was delivering a drug and alcohol awareness presentation in a secondary college, when at question time, a student asked me what it was like to smoke marijuana. I was a little taken aback by the question as I had three police officers sitting nearby as they were to follow my presentation with a message on the scourge of drugs and alcohol in our community, from a policing perspective. My mind flashed back to the most recent times where I had been smoking marijuana, just prior to the beginning of my illness. And this was my answer,

"I used to get home from work (I was somehow managing to hold down a full-time office job) and I would smoke bong after bong until I lay semi-conscious, like a zombie, on the couch. I would then get incredible 'munchies' and eat disgusting food and go to bed feeling sick...What was I thinking? This wasn't fun. I was just addicted."

The other sad side to this story was that I was actually doing much of this alone. Although marijuana had opened the door to drugs for David, after he had moved on to using heroin, he had completely stopped smoking marijuana. On weeknights, as I lay slumped on the couch, stoned out of my head, David usually quietly put away about half a bottle of scotch. Of course when we socialised with friends others often smoked weed with me.

Many say that marijuana is not addictive and it is true that the physical addiction can be overcome fairly easily. However, it is the mental and emotional addiction that can be so difficult to overcome. If my bag of dope was running low, I was straight off to the dealer to buy more. This was addiction.

In the middle of any addiction, regardless of the drug involved, including alcohol, most addicts just can't see what's happening. They lose touch with reality and become so caught up in the drug (or alcohol) scene that they don't even recognise some of the crazy risks they may be taking and just how far they have fallen.

As a bit of advice for drug or alcohol users in this situation, I would suggest the following;

If anyone close to you, whether family or friends, voices any concern for your welfare regarding your substance use, it is time to have a very close look at your situation and where you might be headed. People around us can often see what we can't. This might be the time to reach out for some help. Often it is not until we get out of a substance abuse situation that we can begin to see how serious our addiction had become. To put it simply addiction blinds people to reality. I know this. This was me.

NOTE: I recently came across my specialist's medical notes in which he said, "Her Illness was characterised by many things including acute cardiac and renal failure, complicated by many things, including severe epileptic seizures which led to DAYS in a severe comatose condition, necessitating acute cardio pulmonary resuscitation. She survived." (Because of the coma, I have no recollection of this; however, the indication is that I did actually die… at least once.)

11

The Love of a Mother

"The one who is faithful and true"

Nearly four months into my stay in the Alfred Hospital, I was allowed out again for a day. Mum picked me up to take me for a drive and after spending such a long time 'locked up' and isolated from the outside world, going out felt really weird. I had become sort of institutionalised. The sterile environment, the smell of cleaning chemicals and the endless routines had become 'normal' to me and stepping out into the real world hit me hard. My senses were on high alert and the smells and sights of the city actually made me nervous. Everything was so loud and the people and traffic were moving too fast. I imagined how it must feel to someone who had been locked away for years.

Over the next few hours I gradually became re-accustomed to all of this and at the end of the day we drove to Brighton beach, where we sat in the car and watched the sun go down. It was just mum and me, the woman who had not only brought me into the world, but who had fought so hard to keep me here. A Lou Reed song played on the radio, "Perfect Day".

The day was 'perfect' with my mum by my side. She had been through all of this with me and, as the song infers, I certainly was paying the price for my choices.

What timing, I was alive! After all I'd been through I was still here to enjoy another magnificent sunset and as I listened to the lyrics my heart welled up with emotion. I still get goose bumps when I hear that song.

Mum didn't once mention the drugs or how I got sick. She didn't need to. We both knew. She was just there for me. Despite what she may have been feeling, she showed me unconditional love and that was just what I needed.

What I put my parents through back then, I can only imagine. Through all of this they were both working full time in the family business. My mum showed a love that still amazes me. I know that she couldn't stand the thought of losing her only daughter. When her mother was sick, also in the Alfred Hospital, mum had visited her every day and on the one day that she wasn't able to go, my Nan died. Throughout my long stay in hospital, mum visited me every day and the one day that she rang in to say she was too sick to come in, was the day that I fell into the coma. Mum never missed a day again.

Although I had no doubt that my dad loved me, he really struggled with the whole situation. He was totally shocked that I had been using drugs and so disappointed with me. I guess he had to deal with his own feelings and all of this while still trying to keep the business running.

12

Maternal Instincts

"As dark energy switches back to light"

My stay in hospital had been long and depressing; I was just 25 years old. I went from firstly being not expected to live, to then being upgraded to, "You may have survived but you will be bed-ridden and rattle with pills and probably not live to an old age."

As I lay in a fragile state in my hospital bed it also began to occur to me that I had probably ruined any chance of becoming a mother and I began to ask my doctors about the possibility. Their response was devastating to me, "Kerryn we're very sorry, but with the damage to your kidneys and arterial system and as a result of this damage, your high blood pressure, it would not be possible for you to carry a child." I was shattered. My life was ruined. And to add to the pain, I had done this all to myself. The choices I had made to recklessly follow the crowd and use drugs had caught up with me and now left me feeling devastated and alone.

To make things worse, many of my friends were still out there partying and then there were others who were beginning to settle down and start a family. Feelings of despair overwhelmed me as I lay for months on end in a hospital ward, shockingly thin and weak and with little hope for the future.

I realise that not everyone who uses drugs ends up dead or with a devastating illness and physical scars, but so many do destroy their lives. Of course, there are many who do die each year, either from an overdose or a drug related illness and then there are those who, like me, end up close to death but survive only to be left with permanent scars. There are also numerous people who may use drugs for years or even decades and do not succumb to death or devastating illness, but instead live a life tormented by mental illness or unfulfilled dreams and goals, as addiction drags them down and keeps them from ever achieving anything significant. Using drugs is like playing a game of Russian roulette which is a deadly game of chance. You never know if you will be the one who will get the bullet.

Over the years I have witnessed so many people who have lost or destroyed their lives as a result of drug and/or alcohol use and for every single person who succumbs, I'm sure there are deep feelings of regret that they ever journeyed down that path. As thankful as I am to have survived, I also feel a deep sinking of my heart and even a sense of survivor guilt each time I learn of another drug or alcohol related death or demise.

I must add that despite my foolish choices and the consequences I suffered, my family, my friends and relatives were amazingly supportive and rallied around, willing me to get well. Their love, support and prayers combined with the fact that I usually have quite an optimistic outlook on life, carried me throughout the long hospital stay and depressing medical prognoses.

~~~~~~~~~~

Like most people, I had always thought that one day I would probably meet someone and settle down and have a family. So now with my specialist's prediction that I would never fulfil that dream I became more desperate than ever to have a child of my own. This wasn't the plan. I just wanted to be a mum. However, despite all I have been through, incredibly I have been one of the 'lucky ones'…

I must say that I am a very strong and determined woman, and in the long run this has served me well. Despite having been told that I would never have any children and against my specialist's strong advice, I remained hopeful that I would one day become a mother. By this time I had moved back in with my partner and although I didn't plan to fall pregnant, I did so accidentally, and this turned out to be disastrous. I went to my doctor and when he discovered that I was in fact pregnant, his words were the same as I'd heard before, "Kerryn, with only forty percent function in both of your kidneys, your hypertension (high blood pressure), the medication you are on and the damage to your arterial system, you would most likely not survive a pregnancy and besides a baby probably wouldn't survive either. My advice is that you terminate this pregnancy."

I was devastated. At birth I had been blessed with a strong, healthy body and now, because of my own stupidity, I had seemingly ruined any chance of ever becoming a mother. I took his advice and ended the life that I so desperately wanted to save. I was gutted and I fought back tears for days as I tried to get my head around all of this, while my heart ached for the child I had lost.

So here I was able to fall pregnant and yet not able to carry a baby. I know there are many people who can't have children for numerous reasons and they would absolutely understand the pain that I was now feeling. To make things even worse, I had caused this myself!

But that was not the end of the story. About ten months later, once again I fell pregnant. Again my doctor told me that the risks were far too great, and recommended that I terminate the pregnancy. This time I could not. I decided that the emotional pain was too much, so whatever the risk, I would continue with this pregnancy. At this point David and I were married. Although I tired easily, things continued fairly well with my pregnancy until at 27 weeks (thirteen weeks early) I went into premature labour. With medication my doctors managed to halt this labour and I spent the next seven weeks resting in hospital until at 34 weeks (six weeks early), as predicted, my kidneys began to fail. I had an emergency caesarean section and our beautiful son Kyle was born. It was touch and go for him for a while but we both survived. My obstetrician, Professor Bill Walters, who delivered Kyle, performed a vertical incision (rather than the more common horizontal incision) so that he could look directly at my kidneys from the inside. The report from this confirmed the results of previous tests. Professor Walters said that both of my kidneys were so shrivelled and scarred that I would need a transplant one day. He said my kidneys looked like small walnuts.

Over the next few years, quite miraculously, my kidney function improved just enough for me to carry and give birth to another precious son and a daughter, Stefan and Phoebe. They were also delivered early by C-section, four weeks premature and three weeks premature respectively, but this time not because of severe kidney failure, but as a precaution because of my medical history. My three beautiful, amazing children are now 32, 29 and 26 and given the circumstances, I feel that I am the most blessed woman on the planet!

One of my three precious children has been mildly affected physically because of my drug related health issues; a fact that I will regret until the day I die. However, I am so proud to say that despite the difficulty this has caused, this particular child has worked hard to overcome the obstacles brought on by these setbacks and has achieved so much; a powerful testament to the human ability to overcome. My two other amazing children have also gone on to be real achievers and none of my children have ever touched illicit drugs.

On another good note, although they now all know about my past, my three children have only ever known me as a Mum who doesn't drink, smoke or use illicit drugs. And while the combination of my damaged kidneys and consequently the medication I take, affect my energy levels, I have worked hard to be the best Mum I can be and I love my three children endlessly.

~~~~~~~~~~

During my stay in the maternity ward, I witnessed the unfolding of another really sad drug-related story. As mentioned, when I was 27 weeks pregnant with Kyle I went into premature labour. As previously stated, my doctors managed to halt this but given my massive medical history, they decided not to take any chances and put me into hospital to rest until my delivery. I was admitted to the maternity ward in the Queen Victoria Hospital, Melbourne. The ward was huge. It was a long room with about twenty beds and had an adjoining veranda with another six. This ward was filled with women with all types of high risk pregnancies. In particular there were a number who were there because of drug dependence. Jess was one of these women. She was a very likable girl with a family who adored her, but she had an out-of-control heroin addiction. She was on methadone at the time but still could not help herself. Apparently her family had tried everything to help her. (Of course this could involve any drug of addiction.)

Jess was allowed to leave the hospital occasionally. One night when she was about eight and a half months pregnant she was caught on Television camera on Fitzroy Street, St. Kilda, soliciting. This was aired on A Current Affair with host, Mike Willesee. She had told the reporters that she was trying to make money to buy clothes for her baby, but all who knew her recognised that this was not the case as her mother was to have custody of her baby. When Jess's baby boy was born, she gave him the nick-name E.T. This was because, as a result of her addiction, his skin was too big for his body and he looked very wrinkly. This poor little man had to be slowly weaned off the heroin with the use of morphine so that he would not die from the ravages of withdrawal; a shocking and all too common occurrence.

Two years later there was another report on A Current Affair. Jess' baby boy was now a cute little blonde toddler but the report was not about him. Sadly,

Jess had fallen asleep while smoking a cigarette and died when the house she was in burned down. One of the side-effects of heroin is that it causes the user to 'nod-off'. I have no doubt that this is probably what happened to Jess, causing her to drop her cigarette and set the house on fire. Another precious life wasted because of the evil force of drugs!

A picture of innocence - me with my brother David

With my first cat, Bimbo

Standing by the tent, camping at Ulupna Island, on the Murray River

As a teenager, with my brothers, David and Ian

Water Skiing

My first horse, Tokay

My second horse, Heirarchy (Rarky)

The view from our rooftop in 'Pig Alley', Kathmandu

Me in Kathmandu with a Canadian tourist

The streets of Kathmandu, Nepal - 1976

The magnificent snowy peaks, Pokhara, Nepal

Locals selling their produce on the banks of the Irawaddy River, Burma

We must have been a bit heavy for our rickshaw, poor guy

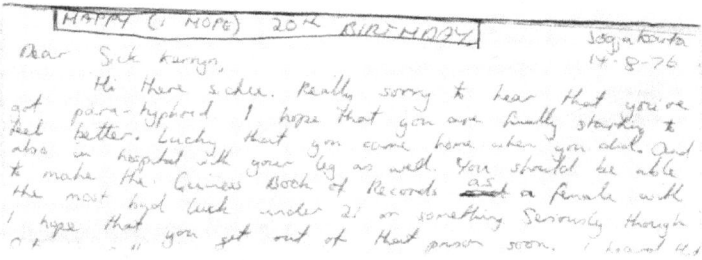

Aerogramme from Vicki, in Jogjakarta, to me in Fairfield Infectious Diseases Hospital dated 14/8/76

...Front of Aerogramme with stamp from 1976

Living in Black Rock - party days

Our very spoilt and not so good watch dog, Mandu

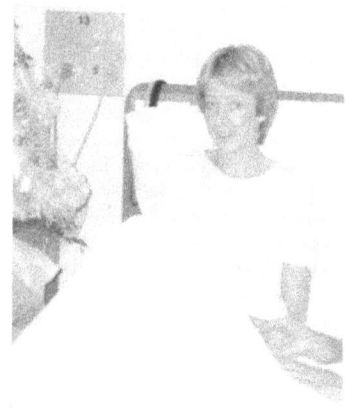
Me, very sick in the Alfred Hospital, 1982

After nearly 5 months in hospital and getting stronger - with my Weimaraner, Eva

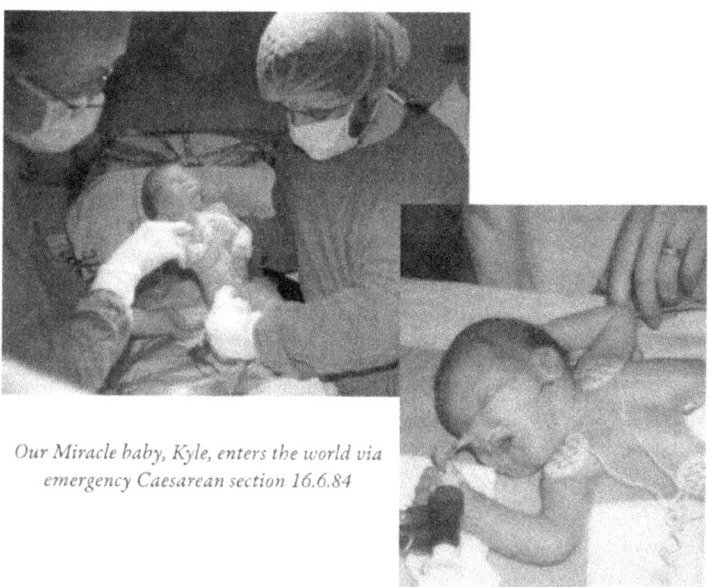
Our Miracle baby, Kyle, enters the world via emergency Caesarean section 16.6.84

Our little man in the neo-natal ward

Kyle, now a healthy little boy...love that 80's hairstyle!

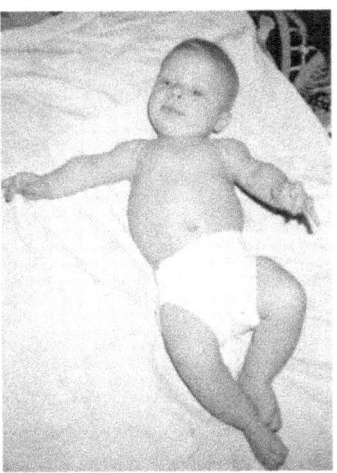

Our miracle baby number two, Stefan

Stefan, a healthy little 5 year old

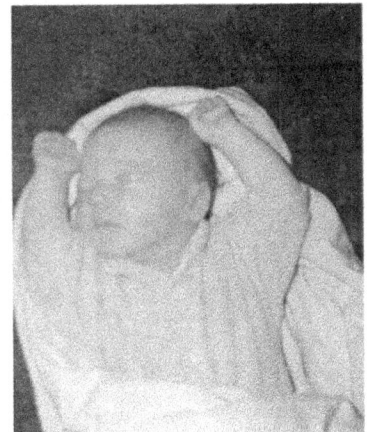

Our miracle baby number three, Phoebe

Our fit, energetic little girl, Phoebe

Me, horse riding again!

Our three 'babies' all grown up

Kyle, Stefan, Phoebe and me

Stefan & his wife Alexandra

Phoebe the Hairdresser

Kyle and his son Gabriel

Stefan and Alexandra

13
Living with the Enemy (2014) - Marijuana

"In a land of bumper sticker opinions"

Another topic I don't remember learning anything about in my youth was that of the immaturity of the adolescent brain and the link to risk-taking; an important issue that can be the catalyst for teenage risk-taking and often perpetuates the use of alcohol and other drugs and other incredibly dangerous behaviour in general.

We now know the scientific fact that the human brain does not fully mature until at least the mid to late twenties. (Although reports from a study conducted in London, dated 2010, claim that the brains prefrontal cortex continues to change well into middle age!)[19] It's

---

[19] http://www.telegraph.co.uk/news/health/news/8204782/Brain-only-fully-matures-in-middle-age-claims-neuroscientist.html - Richard Alleyne, Science Correspondent The Telegraph UK - December 16, 2010

all formed, but softer and more malleable and in that state, far more susceptible to injury, re-wiring or to addiction.[20] The human brain matures unevenly from the back to the front and the last part of the brain to fully mature is the area called the pre-frontal cortex. When adolescents and young adults drink alcohol, smoke marijuana or use other drugs, they can and often do cause permanent damage or rewiring to this area of the brain!

In 2014 I had the amazing opportunity of being featured in a television documentary called 'Living with the Enemy' which aired on SBS (Australia), the topic being 'Marijuana' - The debate on legalisation. I was on the negative side of the debate.

While everyone is entitled to their opinion (and I do understand both sides of the debate), I base my opinion on several factors; first-hand experience - past and present; the scientific evidence on the potential harms of marijuana use; and information coming out of Colorado where it has been legalised.[21] [22]While it is clear that we already have a huge issue with marijuana use world-wide, current information indicates that over

---

[20] http://www.npr.org/sections/health-shots/2014/02/25/282631913/marijuana-may-hurt-the-developing-teen-brain - by Patti Neighmond -NPR Health News - March 3. 2014

[21] http://www.poppot.org/ Parents Opposed to Pot - Regular updates by various reporters.

[22] http://www.poppot.org/2017/06/09/marijuana-through-the-eyes-of-a-doctor/ by Brad Roberts MD - POP - June 9, 2017

time the legalisation of marijuana would greatly increase the number of users.

It's pretty clear to see that with every other addictive substance or behaviour that has been legalised, authorities are struggling to stay in control. For example: alcohol, cigarettes, gaming machines or Poker machines. Consequently these addictions are causing much pain and devastation in the lives of individuals and communities right across this nation.

When I was growing up gaming machines (or the "Pokies") were not legal in the state of Victoria. In 1992 they were legalised in Victoria and in just 25 years, their impact has devastated millions, creating gambling addictions that are tearing apart families across the state. There are now campaigns and advertisements across the media and throughout gaming facilities warning of the harm caused by gambling and promoting "gamblers help lines" etc. Recently a new ad campaign has been running aimed at warning teens about gambling issues related to football, "Love the game not the odds" is the catch phrase. I believe the Government has manifestly shown that it cannot legalise and successfully regulate addictive substances or activities. It also seems that we humans cannot control ourselves when it comes to open slather of legalised addictive substances or activities.

The following is a headline from the Age Newspaper July 24, 2016:

Victorians' poker machine losses rise to $2.6 Billion
By Richard Willingham

Victorians have lost $2.6 billion on the state's poker machines in the past 12 months, $44.7 million more than the previous year,...[23]

~~~~~~~~~

Regarding Marijuana, another obvious issue is that legalising marijuana would not completely eradicate the illegal growing and selling of the drug. Criminals would continue to sell their clandestine products to avoid paying taxes. In other words, we would then have two levels of marijuana distribution to deal with, both legal and illicit. The black market would still exist, just as it does in Colorado.
*** See Appendix for supporting reports.

However, I believe the strongest evidence against the legalisation of Marijuana to date, is found in the following report:

2016 United Nations World Drug Report:
Continual monitoring of new cannabis policies is recommended...

---

[23] http://www.theage.com.au/victoria/victorians-poker-machine-losses-rise-to-26-billion-20160724-gqch5g.html - by Richard Willingham - The Age Victoria - July 24, 2016

Although it is still too early to evaluate the impact of new cannabis policies, the evidence collected to date in the United States points to an increase in cannabis use in states where referendums have led to the legalization of recreational marijuana use. New challenges have emerged in some states of the United States (notably Colorado), including the marketing of unregulated cannabis products (edibles) with a high content of tetrahydrocannabinol (THC). Moreover, there is evidence of an increasing number of cannabis users driving under the influence, as well as an increase in cannabis-related emergency room visits and hospitalizations. However, cannabis-related arrests and court cases related to cannabis offences have decreased. All of these outcome measures would need to be rigorously monitored and evaluated over a period of time before a final assessment can be made.[24]

Naturally the cannabis related arrests and court cases related to cannabis offences would have decreased as cannabis use is no longer illegal in these states.

And finally on the topic of legalisation, just as a reminder, prescription medications, which are 'legal' drugs, reportedly lead to more deaths from overdose

---

24

https://www.unodc.org/doc/wdr2016/WORLD_DRUG_REPORT_2016_web.pdf - Marijuana -UNODC (United Nations Office on Drugs and Crime) -Conclusions and Policy Implications - page XXV than all illicit drugs combined,[25] clearly supporting the argument that drug legalisation does not save lives.

~~~~~~~~~

The complete *'Living with the Enemy'* documentary (which is still available on-line) contained six episodes covering six different 'hot' topics, and the theme was for two people from opposite sides of each particular debate to live in each other's homes for five days; ten days in total. We did not know who our opponent would be until we arrived at their home.

I was flown up to Coolangatta, Queensland and then driven south into Northern New South Wales to a small, well known town called Nimbin[26], where I met my opponent, Michael Balderstone. I like Michael, but strongly disagree with him on this topic.

Michael is the leader of the H.E.M.P. (Help End Marijuana Prohibition) political party and is arguably Australia's number one advocate for legalising marijuana. Michael believes that recreational marijuana should become legal in this country for people over the age of 18. However, as a former drug user who has seen the destruction caused by marijuana and other drugs,

---

[25] https://www.psychologytoday.com/blog/wicked-deeds/201404/prescription-drugs-are-more-deadly-street-drugs - by **Scott Bonn, Ph.D. - Psychology today - April 18, 2014**
[26] *Nimbin is a small country town in a beautiful part of Northern NSW, which is also unfortunately known as the 'Drug Capital of Australia'*

and who also sees the possibility of that going horribly wrong, I strongly oppose legalisation.

Michael's home is situated on a picturesque bush hippie commune just out of Nimbin and a small, rustic bungalow became my home for the duration of my stay. Over the following days Michael introduced me to others who supported his side of the debate and then Michael, all of the camera crew and I flew back to Melbourne where he stayed in my home. When in Melbourne I introduced Michael to people who supported my side of the debate.

There was approximately 100 hours of filming in total, which was then edited down to a one hour program, so as you can imagine, it was pretty full-on!

One of the people I had lined up for Michael to meet in Melbourne was a Professor of Clinical Neuroscience, Prof Murat Yucel. Professor Yucel had been working for ten years on the first of any world studies into the effects of marijuana on the brain. In particular he was conducting a study into an area of the brain called the hippocampus, which is located on both sides of the brain, and he was measuring the size of this area. The plan was to take an MRI scan of Michael's brain, and then to compare the 'Hippocampal volume' with the results from brain scans of people of similar age and background to Michael. [27]

---

[27] *The hippocampus is a major component of the brains of humans and other vertebrates. Humans and other mammals have two hippocampi, one in each side of the brain. The*

Chasing After The Wind

Michael agreed to the scan and when the result came through, on the 10th day of the experiment, we were shown a computer image of a range between two lines where the majority of the brain scans results fell. Anything sitting within this range was considered normal, the higher within the range being the better result. There were approximately 100 other samples of different individual's hippocampal volumes to compare Michael's scan with. According to the report Michael's result fell at the lower end of the normal range, well below the majority of the others, with only a few sitting below his on the screen image. It was right there before our eyes, so there was no doubt. Michael's hippocampal volume was well below average.

It is important to note that Michael stated that he didn't start smoking marijuana until he was 24 years old. In other words, his brain was closer to being fully mature and yet his scan results seemed to indicate significant reduction in his hippocampal volume. In light of this, according to the studies being done, had Michael begun to smoke as a teen or even into his early twenties the result would possibly have been far worse. This then, may have been more evident in his mental capacity and behaviour etc.

---

hippocampus belongs to the limbic system and plays important roles in the consolidation of information from short-term memory to long-term memory, and in spatial memory that enables navigation.

To his credit, Michael did acknowledge that if marijuana were to be legalised, we would need to educate young people on the dangers of using marijuana before the brain was fully mature, i.e. anyone under at least 30. However, if legalised, I'm sure policing this would be near impossible. Michael stated that he believed the explanation for the result of his smaller hippocampal volume was, "Perhaps mine was always smaller." Unfortunately the evidence actually being found from the study indicates otherwise.

While Michael was in the MRI machine having the scan, I asked the Professor about other areas of the brain like the pre-frontal cortex and he replied, "Yes we know about the impact marijuana has on that area, but there is also another area of the brain being studied called the Cerebellum. We already know that this area can be adversely affected by drinking alcohol and current studies are now finding that marijuana can also cause significant changes to this area of the brain."

In other words there are at least three regions of the brain that we do know of at this stage; the pre-frontal cortex, the hippocampus and the cerebellum, that can be and often are permanently altered (re-wired) or damaged by using these potent, mind-altering and addictive substances.

These areas of the brain are responsible for some very important functions including: reasoning, impulses, emotions, memory, reward centre, decision making, motivation, motor coordination, and the ability to learn. We only get one brain. It is so important to protect it. I would urge the reader to really think about this!

Also included in this episode was the following comment by Professor Yucel :

"One of the things that's in the literature at the moment is that if you use cannabis, you double your risk of psychosis"

With the enormous number of individuals already suffering from different forms of mental illness globally, this is a frightening thought.

On the topic of legalisation and Michael's side of the debate, it is also important to note that according to Michael, as recorded on the documentary, he smokes only a few home-grown marijuana joints a day and some days none at all.

In another example, I was recently flying into Dallas International Airport, Texas, and I was sitting next to a 70 year old Texan who told me that he had suffered from PTSD[28] since returning from the Vietnam War. He said that as a result, he had struggled to sleep at night and he found that smoking one marijuana joint each night helped him to relax and sleep well. (Of course there are other equally successful medicinal or herbal treatments available). My response to him was, "If that was all that most people were using marijuana

---

[28] *Post-Traumatic Stress Disorder - A tragic and all too common reality for those who have been involved in active service or those who have suffered trauma of any kind.*

for, I would not be working so hard to warn of the dangers. However, unfortunately, many young (and older) people using weed today, smoke bong after bong of hydroponically grown marijuana. Or they smoke cannabis from plants that have been selectively bred to greatly enhance the level of THC, thus producing a far stronger effect and potentially causing more damage by comparison. Or they may use some more recent popular methods of inhaling marijuana oil, called 'dabbing'[29] or vaping, using vaporisers or e-cigarettes, all of which can and often does lead to harm." My Texan friend then commented that he now understood my stance and why I was speaking out.

Regarding Michael's marijuana use, what this infers is that although Michael's brain scan results pointed to the possibility of marijuana-induced harmful alterations, by all indications, the highly potent products people are smoking or ingesting today will be even more harmful. A horrifying thought.

It's clear to see that this information must be passed on to young people across the nation and the globe in order that they might be fully informed and empowered to think carefully about the choices they will make.

~~~~~~~~~~

---

[29] *Dabbing is inhaling the vapours from a concentrated form of marijuana made by an extraction method that uses butane gas. It is more potent than conventional forms of marijuana because they have much higher concentrations of the psychoactive chemical tetrahydrocannabinol, or THC, than is found in regular cannabis.*

Chasing After The Wind

One other comment I want to make at this point is on the topic of 'medicinal' marijuana. This is a totally different issue to that of 'recreational' marijuana.

Of course I have absolute compassion for anyone suffering from any kind of illness or diagnosis and it is my opinion that marijuana should be thoroughly, scientifically tested and trialled for any possible medical benefits in the same manner that any other medication is trialled. It would be wonderful to discover any of the potential health benefits of the cannabis plant.[30] However, I am not convinced that 'back yard' doctors distributing these products, is a safe practice. Apparently 'back yard' 'medicinal' marijuana randomly tested in Colorado recently, revealed a number of concoctions containing high levels of THC (tetrahydrocannabinol) rather than just the CBD's (cannabidiols) they are claimed to contain. THC is the potent psychedelic component in a cannabis plant that causes a person to get high; it is also the component which can damage or re-wire the brain and can lead to psychosis.[31]

It is also important to note that medicinal marijuana is not a 'cure-all'. With all of the recent hype around this topic, many may misunderstand this important fact. The evidence to date indicates that some health

---

[30] *The legal clinical trials on the use medicinal cannabis have just begun in Victoria, Australia. -2017*
[31] http://www.nbcnews.com/storyline/legal-pot/legal-weed-surprisingly-strong-dirty-tests-find-n327811 - Blair Gable - NBC News - March 23, 2015

conditions may benefit from the use of medicinal marijuana and I absolutely support further in-depth scientific studies to search for as many health benefits as possible. But caution must be taken as there have also been instances of medicinal marijuana treatment actually having an adverse effect on patients.

Professor Milton Cohen, a specialist in rheumatology, in speaking on the field of pain management has warned of Australian governments,` "Reacting to community enthusiasm over science, in legalising the prescribing of medicinal cannabis, generating a culture of 'false hope.' The cart is well ahead of the horse on this one," he said.[32]

In another tragic example, two U.S. women recently died after using medicinal marijuana that contained a deadly fungus.[33]

It is clear to see that medicinal marijuana must go through all the rigorous testing and trialling that is usually applied before the public release of any medication.

*** See appendix for supporting reports.

I believe it is also being strongly pushed by those who see the legalisation of medicinal marijuana as a stepping-stone to legalising 'recreational' marijuana.

---

[32] http://www.heraldsun.com.au/news/victoria/medicinal-cannabis-benefits-still-unclear-pa   Grant McArthur Herald Sun May 13, 2017 pg 4

[33] www.heraldsun.com.au - by Renee Viellaris - Friday May 12, 2017 Pg 9

Another example of the need for extreme caution to be taken in this area.

~~~~~~~~~

On the topic of psychosis, I personally have close friends who have children, in varying age groups, who have suffered severe marijuana induced psychosis. No family is immune to the possibility of their child being affected by drugs or alcohol.

A few years back I took a very good friend's daughter to a Hospital Psychiatric ward for assessment as she had been suffering from marijuana induced psychosis. While in the examination room this fragile young woman burst into erratic psychotic behaviour as her confused mind struggled to deal with the situation. It was so sad to witness and she was immediately restrained by the four medical team members present, sedated and then admitted into the ward where she stayed for several months. What a tragic outcome for a beautiful and much loved young woman.

People affected by marijuana induced psychosis, often only recover if they abstain from using marijuana completely. Continued use of marijuana commonly sets off further psychotic episodes, and sadly some never fully recover. The big problem with marijuana induced psychosis is that no one knows if it will affect them in this manner, until it happens.

On Monday April 20, 2015, I saw two very interesting reports that aired on television. The first was on the evening news where a group of 'Pro-marijuana legalisation' supporters were holding a 'peaceful' protest in the Flagstaff Gardens in Melbourne. Sitting around smoking joints and bongs their arguments were along the lines of, "We should be free to choose whether we smoke marijuana or not;" and, "This drug is not harmful." "Legalise, legalise…" etc.

That same night at 9.35 on ABC TV, the program 'Q&A' aired and a well-known Australian comedian, Dave Hughes, was on the panel. At one point the topic was on mental health issues and Dave spoke up. He said that when he was 21 years old he had begun to have some 'episodes' at night and he then said he began to feel like he was becoming "schizophrenic".

As difficult as it was for him, Dave said he went to his mum and told her what he had been experiencing. Her reply was, "You will need to see a doctor," and she went with him to see a G.P.

Dave stated he then admitted to the G.P. that he had been drinking alcohol heavily and smoking a lot of marijuana and the doctor advised him to stop smoking marijuana. Dave went on to say that at the age of 21 he stopped smoking marijuana and drinking alcohol and has not touched either substance since. His recovery from depression and psychosis followed. He then said, "I don't drink at all. I think the toughest man at the pub is surrounded by a group of drinkers and says, 'no, I'll be right'," he said.[34]

Clearly you don't have to drink alcohol or use drugs to have a good time. Dave has since gone on to be an extremely successful comedian. He has been very brave in sharing his mental health experience, particularly as an encouragement for other sufferers to reach out for help. Dave commented that from the moment he reached out for help, his recovery began.

How different these two stories were that aired on Melbourne Television that night. Three clear observations can be seen from these examples. Firstly, marijuana is not a harmless drug and can lead to depression, psychosis or schizophrenia. Secondly, seeking help can be the beginning of recovery from mental illness or addiction for that matter. And thirdly, life can be amazing without drinking alcohol or using drugs.

*** It is important to note that as far as we know, with the information at hand, it seems that these symptoms are less likely to occur in people who begin to use marijuana moderately after the age of 30. Although other related health issues like lung damage or lack of motivation and unfulfilled dreams etc., may still exist.

---

[34] http://www.mamamia.com.au/dave-hughes-mental-health/ - Mamamia News - April 21, 2015

Harvard psychiatrist Dr. Bertha K. Madra made the following very powerful and significant statement on Marijuana :

"THIS IS NOT A WAR ON DRUGS, IT IS A DEFENSE OF OUR BRAINS"

14
Recollections & Regrets - (2016)

"The curtain coming down"

It's amazing how certain events can trigger memories and emotions years beyond the actual episode. We human beings are such intricately designed creatures. Despite the years that have passed and the incredible trials and blessings I have since experienced, there are still incidents that arise out of the blue and shake me to the core.

The recent news of the sad passing of British rock legend David Bowie set off one of these reactions that absolutely took me by surprise. But in retrospect, although very saddened at his passing, I can now see that this was most likely part of a combination of events that tipped my emotions.

Just a few weeks prior to his death (on January 10, 2016), I had been searching for something I needed down the very back of the shelving in my garage when I came across a small plastic bag containing four used syringes and a smear of dried blood. They had obviously been left there by my now ex-husband, David, several years before. Clearly he had been trying to hide them as he battled the demons of addiction, while desperately trying to appear to live a normal life. He was not proud of this struggle and continually tried to deny his drug use, but this is just how it is with addiction. Of course, I know this well, from my own past drug use.

I must add that overall my husband, David, was not a bad person. He loved our three children and even took pleasure in buying me small gifts for no particular reason, from time to time. But his addiction was like a ball and chain around his ankle that continually dragged him back into the darkness. My husband was one who had suffered past emotional trauma, and opiates had become his pain-killer; a powerful catalyst that often leads to addiction.

There were many times over the years where he managed to break free from his drug use and he worked hard and life in our little family became 'normal' for a while. As previously mentioned, I have an optimistic personality and these times brought with them feelings of cautious hope for the future. But then once again, I would start finding syringes and the arguments would start, the despair would follow and the cycle continued. On the recent discovery of these four syringes, I felt my insides tighten and I think I just went into shock, shutting those emotions down until the following occurred…

At the news of the 'sudden' death of Bowie a flash of memories returned taking me to a time years ago when my husband and I had been re-painting** our home in Black Rock, both of us stoned on heroin, while Bowie's famous hit about 'Major Tom' the junkie, pumped through the house. I was in a place where I had been sucked into the lie that this lifestyle was normal, even cool and totally oblivious to the disasters and devastation that lay ahead.

But now years on with this fresh recollection, triggered by the combination of finding the syringes and the death of Bowie, came that familiar feeling of immense regret as the whole of my journey resurfaced. Memories of my first smoke of marijuana, more drugs, the overdoses, the fights over drugs and money, being robbed by so called friends (who were also drug addicted), my near death, the scars that illness left, my child being affected and the demise of my marriage because of my husband's addiction, flooded my mind.

Of course the news of Bowie's death came as a shock to people across the globe as he had secretly been fighting his battle with cancer. This just happens to be the story of how I was impacted by his death. Yet another trigger that took me back to the deep regrets of the choices I had made in my teens.

I've heard the analogy of human emotions being compared to an onion, where the layers are gradually peeled away as we deal with different wounds and head toward inner healing. I suppose another layer had now been removed. Along with this came yet another level of forgiveness. Just when you think all is forgiven and long gone, a memory is sparked to remind you that there is still a little more to process. I know we all make mistakes that we regret, but this is one that has affected my entire life. I dare say my former husband most likely regrets that first time he ever used a drug as well.

On the topic of forgiveness, it has been said that "carrying un-forgiveness is like drinking a cup of poison and expecting the other person to die." In fact, psychologists have long since discovered the damaging effect that carrying un-forgiveness can have on a person's physical, mental and emotional health. Bitterness eats away at the soul. Forgiving anyone who has ever wronged or hurt you and forgiving yourself is essential in the journey to inner healing. It doesn't mean that you forget everything, or that what's happened is ok, it just means you can start to let go of the pain and begin to move forward with your life. The choice to forgive actually gives you a sense of power over a situation that may have previously left you feeling powerless. And of course in my case, as one who had used drugs in the past, I fully understood the controlling power of addiction.

**In a weird coincidence, right at this moment I am re-painting my current home and secretly over the next few days, having heard this news, I shed a few quiet tears, desperately saddened by Bowie's death but also as I now see releasing another level of pain from my past, as these two incidents and memories collided.

I guess the message in this recollection is that the emotional pain and scars from drug use and all that involves, can remain with you and resurface years after you have overcome addiction. I sincerely hope readers will take note.

The lyrics from 'Ashes to Ashes' by David Bowie, released way back in 1980, are a stark warning about the horrors of drug addiction, a reality experienced by him, even back then...

Bowie sings about desperately wanting to "come down" from the drug and how he is "hitting an all-time low", followed by a warning to stay away from heroin.

According to Amanda H from Metro Lyrics, "This is an autobiographical song by David Bowie that finds him fresh out of a heavy drug use, and his reflection on the man he was during that time."

15

The Other Side of the Story

"Through the headwinds, at the crossroads"

So now to the topic I think I've been avoiding. The one I opened this book with. It's hard to write about someone who was a part of your life for so long without appearing to be bitter or vengeful. But this is not about that. The furthest thing from my mind is to blame anyone else for the negative things that have occurred in my life. I made bad choices and I suffered the consequences. Besides, as previously mentioned, I have long since forgiven myself and all others for the behaviour brought on by our drug use and abuse. The simple fact is drug addiction or addiction of any kind, changes people and leads to covering-up, sneaking, hiding evidence and then feelings of guilt and shame and consequently affects and controls the behaviour of the addict and subsequently the lives of those around them.

I have lived with drug addiction from both sides. Firstly battling with addiction myself (which leaves me in no position to judge anyone else) and secondly, having overcome addiction, I have had years of first-hand experience of living with an addict. My personal drug use covered a total of seven years. My husband continued to battle addiction on and off for another 26 years beyond the time that I stopped using. My only purpose in touching on this side of addiction is to use my knowledge from both angles as a warning to others of the life and soul-destroying power of drug use and abuse.

As mentioned earlier, addiction turns normal, intelligent, loving human beings into hollow souls driven by a need to keep a certain chemical balance and emotional feeling in the body and mind, and in the process causes them to behave in a manner totally removed from normal behaviour.

And then there are the 'normal' times, where they regain control of their 'senses' and function relatively well. This was the reality I lived with. I had a man who desperately wanted to be a good husband and father and to work hard and provide for his family, but the lure of opiates (heroin) is powerful and the battle between 'normal' life and addiction continued. (Of course this behaviour could involve any drug of addiction).

Now I am not going to sit here and say that I was blameless. I had of course also used drugs in the past, but had stopped using when I almost died of drug related heart and kidney failure. In some ways this made the situation even more difficult. I understood addiction and the desire to feel good so this position I found myself in was also massively tormenting. However, as time passed, I went way beyond those feelings and desires as I began to see from the outside the devastating and controlling force of these powerful chemical substances.

Within the marriage I felt tormented in not being able to stop the continued drug use by my husband, and consequently my reactions were not always rational. It is so difficult to behave rationally in an environment that in fact is not rational; where someone is blinded by what they're doing and its impact on those around them. But this is drug addiction. And so the cycle continued.

16

The Drugs Triumph

"So down and laid low, past tired and sore"

    I am often asked how I overcame my drug addiction and it's quite simple really. My illness, which included several near-death incidents, combined with firstly, six months of being extremely sick at home followed by almost five months spent gravely ill in hospital, served as a form of rehab for me. When I finally left hospital I was still very thin and weak and it was several months before I began to regain some form of physical strength. I then also had to adjust to living on medication, in particular blood pressure treatment and for a time, heart medication and fluid tablets.

    My scarred kidneys have left me with hypertension and from the age of 25, I have had to take medication to lower this to maintain 'normal' blood pressure and basically to keep me alive. It took several years to find a medication that really suited me without having the side effect of spinning my head out and leaving me totally exhausted.

Unfortunately, my blood pressure is also affected by the weather. I used to put a tourniquet around my arm to hit up drugs. These days I put a blood pressure cuff around my arm on an almost daily basis. I hate that. And of course to this day I continue to tire far more easily than I ever did before I was sick; yet another element that has contributed to my life-long regret of choosing the path that I did.

~~~~~~~~~~

Despite all of this, you may wonder if I was ever tempted to use drugs again. You bet I was! Earlier on, with my husband and other friends still using, I was very tempted ... a few times. The lure of drugs is strong, especially when living in an environment of drug use, and several times (before my children were born), I was torn between the desire to join in and the fear of what could go wrong. The fear won. With my now badly damaged kidneys, I knew that further drug use could easily kill me. As it turned out, my illness had been both a curse and a blessing. It had caused severe damage to my body, but it also prevented me from falling back into the destructive life of drug addiction.

~~~~~~~~~~

Fortunately I had always been very physically active before my illness and, although this was all extremely distressing to me, sitting around feeling sorry for myself wasn't a part of my make-up. As I mentioned earlier, David and I had by this time married and now, a few years after my near death from heart and kidney failure, we were the parents of a beautiful baby boy and life, although tough, continued.

I was now a mum who no longer drank alcohol, smoked cigarettes or used illicit drugs. Ironically, as one who had previously used drugs with reckless abandon, now because of my subsequent kidney damage, I had become extremely sensitive to medications, vitamins and herbs of all kinds. Everything we take passes through the filter system of the kidneys, and to this day, I still need to be very careful of any concoction I may take, regardless of whether it's medication, vitamins or herbs. Taking the wrong supplement can cause me to totally 'spin-out' and to feel like I have been poisoned.

So a few years further on, here I was blessed by this time with two more beautiful 'miracle' children, but living with a man who continued to battle drug addiction. There are so many stories I could tell of events that took place as a result of his addiction, but as this is not about character assassination but rather an illustration of the devastating and controlling effects drug use has on human behaviour, I will only mention a couple. When living with an addict, it is actually as if you are dealing with the drug itself rather than the person, as the force of the drug seems to take on a life of its own.

Approximately sixteen years ago, I was working part-time as a nurse assistant in an Aged Care Facility in the picturesque country town where we lived. As was the norm, if I was at work, it was David's job to drive down the long winding hill from our home to pick our children up from the school bus stop. On this particular day, it had been wild and stormy with bursts of torrential rain and we had swapped cars so that David could pick up our children in my car, the better, more reliable family car. Although I did most of the school runs, this was quite a normal task for David when I was at work and despite his drug issues he had always been dependable with our kids.

About forty minutes after the children should have been collected I received a call from them informing me that their Dad had not arrived. My heart sank. He was usually reasonably punctual regarding school pick-ups and my mind anxiously raced through the possible scenarios. I had to leave my work and head down the steep, winding road, in the pelting rain to pick them up.

I arrived at the bus stop to find our three children, damp, freezing cold and clearly concerned about the absence of their Dad. They quickly clambered into the car and we headed back up the hill and through the township. I was acutely aware that something disastrous may have happened to their father and wanting to prepare them, I said, "You know this is not like your Dad to be so late, he may have had an accident." No sooner had I spoken those words, than we came across the scene of the accident. There was my white Commodore station wagon smashed over a drain, into an embankment and surrounded by police cars and an ambulance. With my heart pounding, I hurriedly pulled over and fired a command at my kids, "Don't get out of the car!" (I can only imagine what the following moments must have been like for them.)

I ran across the road in the pouring rain and stuck my head in the side door of the ambulance and said "I think that's my husband in there." The paramedic asked, "How do you know that?" My reply, "That's my car." It's funny that I still remember those exact words. I stepped into the ambulance and there he was, lying on a stretcher and being attended to by the paramedics. One look at his face and I could see. I knew that look. He was stoned. I used to say I could tell if he had even just waved heroin or any drug for that matter, under his nose. The paramedic said to me, "David looks pretty pale. Why do you think that is?" Well, I wasn't going to 'dob him in'; this could affect all of us. So my reply was, "Well he's just had a serious accident, I guess he's in shock."

I was furious. This man, my husband, had intended to drive down a dangerous, winding road in pouring rain, stoned out of his head to pick up our three precious children. He could have killed them all and himself! It was in fact extremely fortunate that he had not made it down that hill.

I drove the children home and asked them to wait in the car as I raced inside to hide any evidence that David may have left lying around before they came inside. I was continually trying to protect our beautiful 'babies' from his addiction. Unfortunately, I missed one syringe and my daughter found it. All I can say is that I guess perhaps they were meant to know. It would explain a lot for them.

I was so angry at the thought that he could have killed our children that I refused to visit him in hospital and in my distressed state, I screamed at him on the phone and told him that I thought he should, "Get back into the gutter where you belong!" I'm not proud of that, but I was distraught and there was not much training available at the time on how to live with an addict. There still isn't. Families across the globe struggle on a daily basis with the distress of trying to live with loved ones who are battling addiction. It is painful, it is heart-breaking, it messes with your head and believe me; it's not pretty.[35]

And then I had to face all of the people I knew in the small town where we lived and pretend it was just a normal accident. Fortunately for my sanity, there were a few close friends I could tell the whole story to.

---

[35] Today in Australia there is an organisation called Family Drug Help which is a NFP group comprised of people who have had family members suffering addiction of some kind. www.sharc.org.au Helpline 1300 660 068

As it turned out my husband had not used heroin on this occasion. According to him and unbeknown to me, he had been to a doctor to ask for something to help him sleep. He had been given Temazepam. He was not having trouble sleeping. Besides this was the middle of the day and this was just another desperate measure that addicts use to get drugs. He had mixed the Temazepam into a syringe and injected it. He had then taken off in my car to collect the kids but at the end of our road he had fallen asleep behind the wheel then driven straight through the T-intersection and into the embankment. My car was written off as a result.

Of course David didn't intend to harm our children. He loves them. He would have assumed that he was quite capable of negotiating the car down that steep winding road in the pouring rain while under the influence of drugs. This was a road we both travelled along on an almost daily basis. This is drug addiction. It impairs judgement and alters a person's thinking, often making the user feel capable of achieving anything. As clearly indicated in this scenario, nothing could be further from the truth.

I also know this first-hand. I had once behaved like this too. I am not proud to admit this, but I had taken these risks and driven under the influence of drugs and alcohol several times in the past. But that was long ago. Now through clear eyes, I could see the danger this posed and as our children were involved this time, I couldn't handle it and another little part of me crumbled.

I don't say this to excuse my past actions, but these days we have ample drug and alcohol road safety education and media campaigns. Today people are well informed and know of the need to have a sober designated driver when any intoxicating substances have been consumed. Unfortunately that doesn't take into account drug users who use substances while alone and then get behind the wheel of a vehicle. Addiction blinds people to reality. The reality is that way too many lives are lost or destroyed as a result of people driving under the influence of mind altering substances; an event that can carry a life-long, devastating ripple effect through families and communities.

As a consequence of this incident, David was left very sore and bruised and had crushed a vertebra in his lower back. He had to wear a back brace for several months. I think this shook him somewhat and he made another attempt at staying away from drugs and our little family slipped back into relative normality for a while; well, our version of normal.

Over the following years the cycle continued as my husband swung between his efforts to be a good father and husband and his battle with addiction. I think if he were to write his account, he may possibly try to blame me somewhat for his inability to overcome his addiction and I'm sure at times my reactions didn't help. But blame-shifting is normal with addiction of any kind. I guess it's a way of easing your own mind of the weight of guilt it must carry. The reality is David was already addicted to heroin when I met him and I had been so naïve about all of this and so caught up in the thrill of living the alternative druggie life-style, that I didn't see this as a warning sign.

Again I feel the need to stress that none of this is said in judgement. This sort of behaviour is typical of anyone suffering from addiction of any kind. Addiction is a very tormenting state for any person to be in. Most addicts hate what they're doing, but without some form of help or intervention, they struggle to overcome it. And of course, many people battling addiction are simply self-medicating in an attempt to block out pain. I have learnt over time to separate the person from the addiction.

Over the years I had convinced David to have some counselling, but he didn't always show up to his appointments and as a result his struggle continued. He even went to rehab twice. His first rehab stint was when our first child was about eighteen months old; he was in a live-in facility where he stayed for a number of weeks, but it didn't help. The second attempt was years later when he went to a facility in regional Victoria. This program, which usually has a fairly high success rate, was meant to be a long-term stay of 12-18 months. Unfortunately after only four months David was told he would have to leave the facility, having been accused of breaking the number one rule. David told me that another resident had sneaked some marijuana into the facility and David was implicated in passing it between others. Although I never asked David specifically, my guess is that he was not involved in smoking the marijuana. From my observations during our time together, his drug of choice was heroin or opiates of some kind."

Once again my heart sank as I had allowed myself to hope that David would complete the program and return to us as a new man; drug-free and ready to contribute to our family as a happy, healthy functioning husband and father. But in a way it was also good to have him home. It had been a tough four months living as a single mother and with my damaged kidneys etc., it was a particularly tiring time for me.

A few years later we moved from our home in the bush back to suburbia and with a new beginning, for some time all went well. Both David and I were working fairly hard but unfortunately he had never fully overcome the desire to use heroin and once again the cycle resumed.

There are so many memories I have from this time. I recall sitting on the floor in my bedroom on several occasions dialling number after number in my search for help of some kind for my husband. Rehabs, counsellors, more rehabs and more counsellors as the overwhelming feeling of desperation and hopelessness filled my soul. Despite the fact that he went through some prolonged periods of doing very well, I came to a place where I found it easier to always believe he was using drugs, even if he may not have been, rather than to trust him and then discover that I was wrong. The pain of that disappointment was just too much. Any trust had completely disintegrated. I guess this was a form of self-preservation.

Finally after a few more years of this, one last incident brought our marriage to an end. David's tired old van had broken down once again and he was borrowing my car. Our baby girl by this time eighteen, had recently passed her driver's licence and was also sharing my car. One afternoon after David had driven my car, I hopped in and as I was about to connect my seat belt clasp I noticed a syringe, the sharp end pointing upwards without a cap on.

I saw red! A few years prior to this my husband had been diagnosed with Hepatitis C and as our daughter was now also driving my car I saw the danger this syringe posed to her. Everything inside of me tightened up and I made my resolve as I marched back to face him. I was very calm, but resolute. My words to him were, "You are now endangering your family. I am going out for an hour, if you are still here when I get back, I will call the cops." He knew I meant this and when I returned, he was gone. It was over.[36]

---

[36] *I also have Hepatitis C antibodies indicating that I too had been infected with the virus at some stage. However, I have been extremely fortunate as I am classed by doctors, as one of the 20% who have 'spontaneously' recovered from the virus. This is a disease that over the past 30+ years has infected millions of*

Once again I will add that I know David did not intend to present any danger to our daughter. When heroin is injected, the effect is immediate and, as I know from my own past experience, the user often forgets where he or she has left the syringe.

By this time I had been beginning to suffer from depression; a consequence of living with an addict. We had already 'separated' in the home and I had visited my GP and had been given an anti-depressant. However, with my damaged kidneys, this really didn't agree with me and I felt totally numb within 24 hours; the medication was meant to take ten days to kick in. I didn't like this numbness, I still wanted to be able to feel and I stopped taking the medication immediately. Now as David left our home, I felt a huge feeling of oppression lift off my home and myself, as an overwhelming sense of relief mixed with deep feelings of defeat set in. This was not the plan I had made for my life. Like most people I had entered into our marriage with the usual hopes and dreams of the 'normal' happy functioning family with a mix of friends, parties, sporting activities, work and a full social calendar.

After we separated I ensured that David's contact with our children continued. He regularly came around

---

intravenous drug users across the world. The good news is that very recently a medication has been developed that claims a 90+% cure success rate. Thankfully, after years of trying various treatments, this new medication has completely eradicated David's illness.

with a movie and a pizza to share with them. I would go upstairs and leave them to spend that time together. Regardless of parent's differences, children need the love and connection with both parents, wherever possible.

I have so many more stories that I could share depicting the despair and heartache of living with and addict, but I think I will summarise by reiterating, "DRUGS DESTROY LIVES!"

For anyone who may be living with the daily, painful reality of having a partner, a child or loved one who is battling addiction of any kind, my advice is; talk to someone. Get some professional help, see a doctor or a counsellor and listen to their advice. Living with this on your own is isolating and depressing and can rule your entire life.

I know David must have felt devastated, a failure, and life for him would have seemed doomed. As it turned out this was the beginning of his long journey to recovery.

By insisting he leave I had actually done him a favour and I'm happy to say that after an initial almost deadly spiral out of control (I'm sure those details could fill another book), David has totally turned his life around; the best possible outcome for him and for our children. Of course he was also left with some physical and no doubt emotional scars, but all things considered, he has been a very fortunate man.

In retrospect, I can see that David was never going to overcome his addiction while living in our family home. In my attempt to help him, I had probably been inadvertently enabling him to continue using drugs. Something drastic had to happen to wake him up. I am not suggesting that everyone battling addiction should be forced to leave the home as each case needs to be assessed individually. This just happened to be the right decision for our situation.

So basically, both David and I only stopped using drugs when we hit rock bottom. For me it was near death and for David it was pretty much losing everything. Without some form of intervention, this is a very typical scenario.

I know there will still be some who read this account and yet think, "That won't happen to me. I will be able to stay in control. I'm just going to have a bit of fun."

For anyone who may think like that, please think again: In 2015 The Sydney Morning Herald reported that in this wonderful nation of Australia, we have double the number of people on rehabilitation waiting lists than we have available spaces, particularly right now as a result of the current ICE epidemic. I would suggest these people reconsider that thought.

Sydney Morning Herald - August 13, 2015
Ice addicts waiting up to three months for rehabilitation
By Sarah Whyte

Ice addicts are facing waiting periods of up to three months to get into rehabilitation clinics, as Prime Minister Tony Abbott described the drug as the "worst drug scourge" Australia has ever faced.

St Vincent's hospitals in Sydney and Melbourne, the Salvation Army and rehabilitation centres in Western Australia and the ACT have all reported waiting times of several months, as they struggle to cope with the demand of people's addiction to methamphetamine.

~~~~~~~~~~

In 2014 I was listening to a talkback show on the Melbourne radio station 3AW. The main topic at the time was methamphetamine or ICE. A young man named Matthew called in and spoke with the host of the day, Nick McCallum. Matt's call was regarding his desperate search for a place in a rehabilitation centre and his distress at the lack of government funding for those who were seeking help for their addictions. Matt said he had been a keen golfer who was playing at a very high standard until the age of nineteen when he entered the 'night club' scene and began to use alcohol and drugs. Over the following months his addiction to alcohol, marijuana and then ice began to spiral out of control. He battled his ice addiction over the next few years until he recognised the damage it was causing and that he desperately needed be free from it.

At the time of his call into 3AW Matt was 32 years old. He had no money left, his girlfriend had left him, he had sold everything he owned and he was living with his grandmother. What Matt had done to overcome his ice addiction is common. As ice is a stimulant drug, the irrational assumption is that by using the opposite drugs (or depressant drugs), a person should be able to get themselves free from the stimulant addiction. So he began to self-medicate with alcohol and marijuana to achieve this. This is all very good in theory, but the problem is Matt, like so many, then became addicted to both alcohol and marijuana. This is why he found himself in desperate need of rehabilitation.

    The radio host asked if any listeners might be able to help Matt, and feeling deeply moved by Matt and his situation, I called in. I left my contact details and Matt returned my call and we arranged to meet in the city. Matt was a likeable young man. He seemed nervous and a bit edgy but he was desperate for help. I put Matt onto a rehabilitation facility that I knew of, and after much encouragement and coercing, (as Matt struggled with his decision to commit to many months in rehab) he finally entered the rehab program.

    I am so pleased to say that Matt succeeded in his battle to overcome addiction and with his life back on track, he is now living and working in far North Queensland, away from his drug connections and once again he is playing his favourite sport, golf. For those who play golf, Matt recently posted on Facebook that his official handicap is now down to 2. That makes him some golfer! What a great achievement. Addiction recovery is possible and many drug and or alcohol users who seek help, do go on to live very productive lives.

UPDATE: August 2017 Matt has just become Club champion at his local golf club! So proud of you Matt!!

Matt has kindly given me permission to use his story because, as one who has suffered the pain of addiction, his words were, "I want to warn others about the horror of drug use and addiction."

17
Why?

"Where souls are downtrodden"

I know there will be those who will wonder why and ask, "If your husband was battling addiction for so long, why did you stay with him?"

Sometimes I still ask myself that question but it's complex and there were several factors that came into play.

Firstly, as I've mentioned a few times now, David was not a bad person. He'd had a tough journey in life and opiates or heroin had become his pain-killer. Big mistake! Secondly, he always loved our children and although, naturally, under the circumstances there were some pretty heated arguments, there was never any violence or physical abuse. However, in retrospect, I can now see that to live with the behaviour of an addict; with the covering up, the missing money etc., is in fact living with a form of mental and emotional abuse, regardless of whether it is intended or not. In our case

I'm sure it was not. I believe David hated his addiction and the trauma it was causing to our family.

There was also the fact that I actually believe in marriage and I had married David "for better or for worse." And as he did have some extended periods where he worked hard and got off the drugs, the hope of a normal life would creep back in.

As I use the word 'normal', I must add that the longer you stay in a particular situation, the more normal it becomes to you. In other words it becomes difficult to imagine a different life or even what a healthy relationship really looks like. This became my normal.

But the most significant reason for staying in the marriage was that it seemed the best option for our children. I am well aware of the devastating impact divorce can have on young children. For the most part David was a 'functioning addict' and in amongst his battle with his 'demons', we still managed to do some normal family things together; trips to the Zoo, the movies, the occasional holiday particularly up north to visit his father and going to his work family Christmas parties etc. I even got back into horse riding, which was a great way to escape the reality I was living with at home. Naturally we both did our best to hide his addiction from our children and from their perspective, particularly when they were younger they were all simply part of a loving, healthy family. Our mutual love for our children never wavered.

To leave the family home with three young children would probably mean moving into a rental property and to struggle on a single parent's income. (As a mum, I always worked part-time too, so despite his drug use, with both incomes we were surviving.)

Then of course there's the fact that I too was a former heroin user and naturally this meant that I fully understood the driving force behind the addiction. So in my mind, who was I to force him out of our home for doing something I had also done in the past? Who was I to tell someone else to stop using drugs, just because I had nearly died and was forced to stop? This dilemma really messed with my head.

But after a time that reasoning wore off as living with an addict tore at my heart, my head and my soul. David was married with a wife and three children. He had responsibilities. The excuses for using drugs had worn thin and now the addiction had become just a desire to get stoned. It was a mental, physical, spiritual and emotional issue. But this is how it is with addiction of any kind. We now know that addiction can rewire the brain and the pleasure centres of the brain causing the user to crave the source of addiction until this craving is satisfied. This is why it is now often classed as an illness or a 'health issue'.

For several years David had functioned quite well, free from drugs and working full-time as a salesman at a large retail store. Being a clever man, he excelled in that role, but over time the drug use crept back in. I'm sure the guilt he carried with this must have tormented him greatly.

I felt trapped in a continuous cycle of emotional highs and lows as our family life swung from relatively normal to out of control. I was very busy raising three children, running a home and working part-time and I guess I just morphed into this lifestyle.

This was also something that I could not easily talk about with others. However, I had one very close friend, Paula, whose husband was battling alcohol addiction and having someone close who understood the trauma of such a situation absolutely brought me (and probably her) some comfort as we were able to 'unload' our pain and frustration, and draw on each other for strength.

I remember clearly the day that I decided I had to cut off my feelings for the man I had married. On this particular evening he was late home from work and I had no idea where he was. This was just before mobile phones were widely available and I had no way of contacting him. I had been down this road before. I'd been filled with the feeling of dread at the thought that he may have overdosed somewhere and I had called all of the local hospital emergency rooms in my search for him. I couldn't do this anymore. It was too much. I was convinced by this stage that he would probably die from a heroin overdose and I had to sever my emotional connection with him. On that day my heart went cold as

I consciously separated my feelings and emotions from my husband. It was all I could do to survive.

It was at this time that I began to have another thought. I was sure by now that David would most likely die from a heroin overdose. It's hard to admit now, but I began to secretly believe that if he was going to die then it would be better for him to be killed in a car accident so that it would be a 'respectable' death. For him to go in this manner, would mean that our children would not have to grow up with the knowledge that they had lost their father to a drug overdose.

I believe most people living in this situation would understand these desperate thoughts. Of course I didn't want my husband to die, but in retrospect, I can see that this was probably a way of preparing myself for the worst. These kinds of thoughts clearly indicate how living with a family member battling addiction messes with you head!

Although I had always tried my best to protect our children from their Dad's battle, by this time they knew. They had found syringes and had heard arguments, but they were still young and didn't know how to deal with all of this. As far as they knew none of their friend's parents had any drug problems, and from what I could tell, none of our precious children had talked to anyone about what was happening at home. It was painful for them and they preferred to see only the good side to their Dad; because there was a good side. The side of a loving Dad, who joked with them, watched movies with them and showered them with small gifts. Our children never felt unloved. And so the charade continued.

I'm sure, as is the case for most people who battle addiction, David never set out to become a drug addict. He had told me that he'd found that at first opiates gave him a sense of 'peace' he hadn't felt in a long time. But unfortunately this was the beginning of a spiral into addiction as the drug not only numbed out any emotional pain but most likely altered the chemical composition in his brain; a very sad and very common scenario. After a time the reason for using opiates changed, and physical and mental addiction to the chemicals took over. Readers please take note.

Very recently David explained to me that his prolonged drug use was brought about by his "need to self-medicate with opiates in his attempt to temporarily lift the overwhelming shadow of Hepatitis C induced chronic fatigue". Allowing him "the strength to function and fulfil the demands of the real world." However, he now reflects on the fact that "one thing leads to another."

*** See Appendix for article on *"The Science of Drug Abuse and Addiction"*

~~~~~~~~~~

In conclusion to Part I of my story I must add that after all of these struggles and desperate times, many years ago I totally turned my life around and I have since been on a wonderful journey as a mother, daughter, partner and friend to many. Although left with some physical scars, I have done my best to make the most of my life. I have enjoyed many and varied part-time employment opportunities. Also horse riding, drawing and painting, re-painting and decorating my home (on a Gumtree budget ☺...I adore pre-loved items) and just spending time with friends. I love sunsets, stormy seas and clear, starry nights and just the privilege of being alive. I guess I am a living testament to the fact that no matter what trials we may go through, there is always hope.

PART II

18
Hope

"From Valleys deep, the mountains to climb"

As I touch on the following few chapters I'd like to remind the reader of a few things:

Firstly, although these chapters predominantly cover the extremely dark side of addiction, I must state that there is always hope for those who seek help. Recovery from addiction is possible.

Secondly, although the impact of drug and alcohol abuse worldwide is huge, according to national surveys, the majority of people do not go down the path of substance use and abuse. I am not suggesting that everyone will end up using drugs and that all is hopeless. Life on this wonderful planet can be amazing and I will touch on the topics of recovery, hope and potential in later chapters.

Thirdly, this is not a comprehensive list of illicit drugs but rather some of the more commonly used substances. For a more comprehensive list go to:

http://adf.org.au/drug-facts/

19

Meth

"Chasing a desperate treasure"

The country of my birth, where I have lived my entire life, is a beautiful country. Australia. It is known as 'The Lucky Country'. Surrounded by sea, filled with vast deserts, rain forests, expansive farmland, picturesque 'Aussie' bushland, amazing wildlife, famous landmarks, both natural and manmade, and vibrant growing cities - Australia has it all. My city, the City of Melbourne, has been named the 'Most Liveable City in the World' for the past seven years in a row and yet like so many great cities there is a dark side, a very dark side!

In 2014 the United Nations World Drug Report announced that Australia has the highest percentage of 'recreational' drug users in the world.[37] We are

---

[37] http://www.dailytelegraph.com.au/news/nsw/australia-comes-top-of-global-list-for-recreational-drug-use-in-united-nations-

considered a wealthy country and as such we pay high prices for recreational (illicit) drugs. Consequently, Australia is a huge target for both international and local drug traffickers.

Over recent years one of the most destructive illicit drugs has made its mark, targeting people of all age groups and in all demographics. This drug is Crystal Methamphetamine, more commonly known as Crystal Meth or Ice.

Crystal methamphetamine ('Ice') is a stimulant drug. This means it speeds up the messages travelling between the brain and the body. It's stronger, more addictive and therefore has more harmful side effects than the powder form of methamphetamine known as speed. Ice can cause some or all of the following symptoms; hyper alertness or nervousness, insomnia, scratching and picking (as users feel the sense of 'bugs' crawling under their skin), racing heart, meaningless repetitive behaviour, grinding teeth, 'meth mouth'[38] and dilated pupils. An ice user often feels aggressively smarter and becomes argumentative, often interrupting other people and finishing their sentences.

2014-world-drug-report/news-story/764732bd5eb5037096389fcd55bfbcab - Andrew Carswell, The Daily Telegraph - July 6, 2014

[38] www.livescience.com/1010-mouth-meth.html/ by Jenna Bryner - Sept 21, 2006

Ice use can also lead to aggression, violence, depression, paranoia and psychosis.

"Psychotic symptoms can sometimes last for months or years after a person has quit abusing methamphetamine, and stress has been shown to precipitate spontaneous recurrence of methamphetamine psychosis in formerly psychotic methamphetamine abusers."[39]

Our hospital emergency wards have become regular scenes of drama, violence and tension as patients are admitted, usually by police, in a state of wild psychosis as a result of using ice.

Early in 2016, I took a friend to a local hospital Emergency Room as he was suffering a medical emergency. As we waited in the cubicle he had been allocated we witnessed the following shocking scene:

Two of the hospital staff walked into the cubicle directly opposite us and proceeded to attach some black strapping to the bed in that cubicle. A few minutes later two police officers dragged a loudly protesting, handcuffed young man into the cubicle. He was approximately 28 years of age. He was then rather forcibly laid on the bed as the black strapping, was attached to him, restraining him at both wrists and ankles. Over the following hour or so, the entire ward

---

[39] https://www.drugabuse.gov/publications/research-reports/methamphetamine/what-are-long-term-effects-methamphetamine-abuse - NIH - National Institute on Drug Abuse - Sept 2013

was filled with his bellowing as this young man roared, hissed, spat, growled and threatened nursing staff and then cried and whimpered as he tried to bargain his way out of the situation.

Obviously, because of privacy laws, the hospital staff members were not permitted to reveal to us the exact cause of his behaviour, but I know enough about these events to say that this man was most likely suffering from ice induced psychosis. We clearly overheard the psychiatric nurse's visit with him as she explained who she was and why she was there. His reaction was to verbally abuse her and threaten her with words like, "F… off" and "I never forget a face!" This shocking behaviour continued until finally the young man succumbed to the sedation he'd been given and he lay 'un-conscious' on his back with his mouth agape.

This was such a sad scenario to witness. This young man was somebody's son, possibly even somebody's father and I dare say when he set out to get high that night, he didn't expect to end up in a Psych ward.

On visiting that same ward a few months later, I was informed by hospital staff that, tragically, this is an all too common occurrence with patients entering the emergency ward suffering drug induced psychoses on an almost daily basis, with the number greatly increasing on a Friday or Saturday night. And once again I will say, everyone thinks it won't happen to them.

~~~~~~~~~

In 2015 NSW Police Commissioner, Andrew Scipione said, "The ice epidemic could bring Australia to its knees and Police will be powerless to prevent it unless the whole community joins the fight." ... Did you catch that? 'The Lucky Country' with a major city regarded as 'The most liveable city in the world', could be brought to its knees by an illicit drug. We have a big problem! In other words, anyone who uses ice is potentially playing a part in the downfall of this wonderful nation. It is a frightening and sobering thought. [40]

The Victorian Government alone has invested a total of $81 million to respond to the scourge of ice, including $57.6 million in the 2016-17 Budget to expand treatment services, protect frontline workers, and make communities safer. [41]

Nationally the figure is far greater. The following is from the Australian Government Department of Health dated 3/7/17: "To underpin the NIAS, (National

---

[40] http://www.dailytelegraph.com.au/ice-epidemic-could-bring-nation-to-its-knees-warns-nsw-police-commissioner-andrew-scipione/story-e6freuy9-1227285222295 - Joe Hildebrand, The Daily Telegraph March 30, 2015

[41] http://www.abc.net.au/news/2017-04-28/victorian-government-announces-funding-to-fight-ice-epidemic/8479002 - Jean Edwards - ABC News April 28, 20167

Ice Action Strategy) the Government has provided $298.2 million over four years from 1 July 2016 to reduce the impacts associated with drug and alcohol misuse to individuals, families and communities."[42]

This shocking news is a clear indication of the depth of the ice problem in Australia.

And yet in the UK this drug is not so popular. Across Britain ice is seen as a 'dirty' drug. It seems that the British people are smarter than much of the Western world regarding methamphetamine use, as they recognise the destruction and chaos this drug can cause; consequently the percentage of ice users in the UK is considerably lower than its Western counterparts.

~~~~~~~~~

I have a few good friends who have a much loved son or daughter who has been caught up in this tragic epidemic and I am often asked to talk with them. Whenever I meet with people who are trapped in this shocking and chaotic cycle of addiction, I always ask what the first drug was that they used and it is almost always marijuana. I know only too well the pattern, the doors are opened, their guard is dropped and next they find themselves in the middle of the drug scene where

---

[42] http://www.health.gov.au/internet/main/publishing.nsf/Content/MC15-009596-national-ice-taskforce

other drugs are always easily accessible and then... they try ice.

I know many would probably have said, "I will just try this once", but ice is an incredibly addictive substance. Crystal Methamphetamine releases such high levels of dopamine[43], that it causes the user to feel indestructible; as if they can 'conquer the world'. They feel super energized, totally freed from the stresses of the world and as if they can achieve anything. But this is the lure. This is a totally chemically induced feeling, one that ceases when the drug has worn off and what follows is a feeling so opposite to the 'super hero' feeling the ice first gave them, that the user crashes into a massively depressive state; so depressed, that they feel a desperate need to get more of the drug. As a consequence addiction can so easily begin.

Regretfully, I admit that I used a lot of speed (amphetamine) years ago and I am very familiar with the extreme 'come-down' and the depressed state that leaves you in. But according to reports, with methamphetamine, those effects are greatly multiplied.

I had one particular episode of speed come-down that led me to an action that I will always regret. I went

---

[43] *In the brain, dopamine functions as a neurotransmitter—a chemical released by neurons (nerve cells) to send signals to other nerve cells. The brain includes several distinct dopamine pathways, one of which plays a major role in reward-motivated behaviour. Most types of reward increase the level of dopamine in the brain, and many addictive drugs increase dopamine neuronal activity.*
https://en.wikipedia.org/wiki/Dopamine

to my older brother's wedding high on speed. I had no intention at all of doing that, but stupidly David and I used speed the night before the wedding. That's what addicts do. They don't consider the consequences of their drug use. The following day we were both feeling so flat, as the chemicals left our system and our dopamine levels struggled to return to normal, that we realised we would never be able to get ready for the big event let alone arrive there on time. We couldn't move. So we had another hit of speed. I was stoned out of my head on speed on one of the biggest days of my brother's life. I so wish I could go back and change that.

As you can imagine, I can barely believe that another drug could have an even more debilitating come-down effect than speed but, as reported, with ice it is far worse. Although both are central nervous system stimulants, and both can be extremely destructive, they have a different chemical composition. Ice is purer, stronger and more addictive and therefore has more even harmful side effects than speed. Ice addiction is so common in this country that right at this moment we are in the grip of what has been labelled an "Ice epidemic". In fact, Australia has one of the highest percentages of ice users in the world! And the reason for that? As mentioned earlier, Australians pay the highest prices for drugs and consequently, Australia is a huge target for drug traffickers, including ice.

A shocking side effect of ice is that continued use can actually damage the dopamine transporters and receptors of the brain as massive amounts of dopamine (>1000% above basal levels) are artificially released.[44] As dopamine works as part of the reward system of the brain, or the 'feel good' area, any damage to this area can be devastating. When an ice user damages the dopamine transporters and receptors, the natural ability to feel happy or contented is affected and the user begins to slip into a constantly depressed state of mind. This in turn drives the user to seek out more of the drug to restore the happy or 'high' sensation and so the cycle continues. At this point of addiction, ice users rarely feel the 'super hero' sensation they first felt and they now find themselves caught in the trap of using the drug in a desperate effort simply to feel 'normal'. Once addiction is fully set in motion, any high they may feel is also now far less in duration. Tolerance has set in. In other words, they need to use more of the drug to feel the same 'high' and as a result they need to 'score'[45] more often.

This is what I call "chasing after the wind". An addict can never hold on to the feeling they are chasing, as the effects of drugs wears off, and so the pursuit continues.

---

[44] https://www.ncbi.nlm.nih.gov/pmc/articles/PMC3042341/ - Michael Allerton, MS and William Blake, MD - PMC Us National Library of Medicine .- Winter 2008

[45] Score - To buy drugs

From here on ice addiction can completely control a person's life. Many ice addicts can't hold down a job and spend their days and nights, doing whatever is necessary to make the money they need to score the drug. Robbery, prostitution, drug dealing and crimes of all kinds are regularly committed by ice addicts desperate to raise funds to score. Tragically, as a result the crime rate in this country and in all countries where ice addiction is prevalent, is on the rise.

Then there are those who say they can use ice and hold down a job at the same time. There are abundant reports of both 'white collar' and 'blue collar' workers using ice while still holding down a job. While this may be true for a period, time and time again it ends up in disaster. The following scenario is so typical of this class of methamphetamine user:

I recently read the account of an ice addict who fell into this class of users. He was an office worker with a highly paid job. He was doing extremely well in his profession, working long hours and making big money, but he made the comment that no one ever queried how he could work such long hours. According to this man, he had been putting in 70-80 hours of work a week and all seemed wonderful, until one day something changed.

The man said that he was driving home on his usual route after a long day in the office when he started to become paranoid. He began to feel that someone was watching him. These thoughts grew and grew in his mind until he was so convinced that someone was spying on him that he believed his car was filled with hidden cameras. The man pulled over and in a wild panic proceeded to tear apart the dashboard of his car in his desperate attempt to locate and remove the (imaginary) bugs or cameras. He then took himself to the police station to report the 'imaginary' crime. This was the beginning of a rapid decline into methamphetamine induced psychosis. Most people, who use ice long term, thinking they have it under control, eventually succumb to the psychotic effects of these potent mind altering chemicals.

This is probably a good time to mention a fact about these chemicals. Ice is a man-made product that contains chemicals that a normal person would never consider putting into their body. Some of those chemicals include:

Acetone - Nail polish remover or paint thinner;

Lithium - Used in batteries;

Toluene - Used in brake fluid;

Hydrochloric Acid - a corrosive, strong mineral acid with many industrial uses;

Pseudoephedrine - decongestant found in cold medicine…

Etc. Etc. And this is just some of the list. Most illicit drugs are poisons. When a person takes one of these substances, the 'high' they are feeling is simply the body reacting to the poisons as it fights to eliminate them. Please think about this!

Because of my own story and past connection to illicit drugs, I am regularly contacted by parents or friends of people who are battling addictions of all kinds. I have recently connected with a number of people suffering ice addiction and have worked hard to help them to get into rehab. What I have witnessed time and again is that although some of these ice users might seem relatively normal to talk to, the constant use of ice has robbed them of the ability to function normally. It has 'hijacked' their brain. It seems that the only thing they can really do well is to score drugs. Their life in general is disjointed, disorganised and chaotic. Everyday tasks have taken a back seat for so long that, combined with the physical damage to the brain [46]*they have forgotten how to exist in the real world. It is scary to think of the number of ice-affected people who are just barely existing in our society; in our local communities, and causing havoc and heartache for their families, friends, neighbours and anyone they might come in contact with. This is a frighteningly destructive drug.*

*** Damage to dopamine transporters is also reportedly connected to impaired cognitive and motor skills. The only possible chance the brain has to recover, is if the addict stops using crystal meth

---

[46]

http://neurosciencefundamentals.unsw.wikispaces.net/The+Brain+%26+Methamphetamine Peter Trikoulis, Michelle Anne, Chloe Starr, Jaclyn Lee - Neuroscience Fundamentals altogether, and then allows the brain a prolonged time to heal, usually at least 6 - 12 months. In other words, it is possible to recover from ice addiction. However, in some cases it may be too late for total healing to occur.

It has now also been reported that ice users have brain changes similar to Parkinson's disease. [47]

People who find themselves in this state of mental, physical and emotional chaos desperately require a prolonged period in an accredited rehabilitation facility to have any chance of restoring their lives. Without this intervention, the risk of backsliding is almost inevitable. Relapse for ice users is so common that most have several attempts at rehab before they fully recover. It is reported that only 2-7% of ice addicts fully recover.

I was recently speaking with a female ice addict as she was about to enter rehab. She told me that a close friend, who is also addicted to ice, had installed security cameras outside the rough makeshift dwelling where he lived. He had recently lost his home, his marriage, a huge amount of money and much more because of his addiction. She said he spent hours watching the security screen as he was convinced that he was being followed. He had also ripped apart the

---

[47] http://www.abc.net.au/news/2017-04-06/ice-users-with-brain-changes-similar-to-parkinsons-disease/8421132 - By Chris McLoughlin Updated 6 Apr 2017

entire dash and console of two of his cars as his ice-induced psychosis had him convinced that his car was bugged. Sadly, all of this this behaviour is typical of ice-induced paranoia and as I have mentioned previously, no one is immune to the possibility of a family member falling into this trap.

For some the psychosis can set in the very first time they use the drug and for others it can manifest further down the track.

Ice use can also lead to overdose. If any of the following symptoms are experienced by a person who has used ice, an ambulance should be called immediately: [48]

- Racing heartbeat and chest pain
- Breathing problems
- Fits or uncontrolled jerking
- Extreme agitation, confusion, clumsiness
- Sudden, severe headache
- Unconsciousness
- Stroke, heart attack or death

Methamphetamine is a dangerous drug, a fact clearly indicated in a recent Australian newspaper article:

---

[48] http://www.druginfo.adf.org.au/drug-facts/ice#sthash.PKK0gF03.dpuf - Australian Drug Foundation

Ice-related drug deaths in Australia double between 2009-2015, study finds

"*Deaths related to the use of ice doubled between 2009 and 2015, with heart disease and stroke emerging as significant causes, a study has found.*"[49]

~~~~~~~~~

Another devastating effect ice can have on users as psychosis hits, is that it can cause the user to become extremely aggressive and violent, causing injury or even death to others. This can happen in person or behind the wheel of a car. There have been numerous tragic incidents of this kind; one of the most tragic being the murder of an innocent ten month old baby boy in the Australian regional town of Bendigo.

A burglar, high on alcohol, marijuana and ice, was in the middle of a psychotic episode, when he randomly broke into the home of a young family and repeatedly bashed the much loved little boy to death as he lay sleeping in his cot, leaving the family devastated. The murder was described in court as "an utterly evil crime" as he had bashed the innocent child over thirty times. The perpetrator, was arrested, and tried by a Victorian Supreme Court judge, who

---

[49] https://www.theguardian.com/society/2017/jul/31/ice-related-drug-deaths-in-australia-double-between-2009-2015-study-finds?CMP=share_btn_tw Australia Associated Press - The Guardian July 31, 2017

sentenced him to a minimum of 32 years in prison. He was only nineteen years old at the time of the heinous crime.[50]

In a shocking revelation in Victoria, there have been up to fourteen ice related murders in as many months; an appalling crime that is on the increase.[51] As indicated earlier, tragically, the rate of death among ice users has also had a rapid increase.[52]

Another shocking revelation in a recent newspaper report, stated that children as young as eleven have been found to be using methamphetamines.[53] Eleven years old! These are children who have not even reached puberty. Something must change.

Ice use is a total mind and soul destroying waste of life!

---

[50] http://www.abc.net.au/news/2014-06-13/harley-hicks-jailed-for-life-over-zayden-veal-whitting-murder/5520514 - ABC News June 14, 2014

[51] http://www.heraldsun.com.au/news/law-order/tide-of-evil-drug-ice-linked-to-killings-of-14-people-in-14-months-across-victoria/news-story/71bb986f268adc9b1939ef836028913f Mark Buttler, News Limited March 27, 2014

[52] http://www.abc.net.au/news/2013-10-14/ice-deaths-skyrocket-according-to-figures-from-victorian-coroner/5021190 - By Jeff Waters Updated 14 Oct 2013 - ABC News

[53]
https://myaccount.news.com.au/heraldsun/subscribe?pkgDef=HS_PDO_P0415A_W04&directSubscribe=true&b=true&sourceCode=HSWEB_WRE170_a&mode=premium&dest=http://www.heraldsun.com.au/news/law-order/primary-school-aged-victorian-kids-addicted-to-drug-ice/news-story/dd5ff9b35539f54979264481d3ea4025&memtype=anonymous

*** See Appendix for reports on Methamphetamines (Ice)

http://www.druginfo.adf.org.au/drug-facts/ice#sthash.PKK0gF03.dpuf

*** Note: Of course there are also other forms of amphetamine such as speed and cocaine, but as mentioned I am not covering all illicit drugs and more can be learned about these substances at:

https://adf.org.au/drug-facts/

19a
A Tribute to Aaron

"And the Angels sing"

Approximately five years ago I received a call from a friend who told me that a close friend of hers had a son who was using ice. This young man was Aaron. I was put in contact with Aaron and he agreed to meet with me and we caught up for a coffee. Aaron turned up wearing a short sleeve T-shirt and it was clear to see that he had been using Ice. His arms in particular were completely covered in small scabbed sores. Aaron had been suffering from one of the shocking side-effects of methamphetamine use, where the drug causes the user to feel the sensation of bugs crawling under the skin.

Another effect of ice, as these potent chemicals flood the brain, is that it can cause the user to engage in repetitive behaviour. With the combination of these two sensations a user can pick or dig continuously at their flesh in an attempt to get the imaginary 'bugs' out from under their skin, often leaving the user covered in sores.

Aaron was a very likeable young man but clearly fully entrenched in the depths of ICE addiction and unable to see just how catastrophic his future could become. Not long after this meeting Aaron became the father of beautiful twin girls and, as much as he loved them, he continued to struggle with his addiction.

He did try rehab and even became free from this insidious drug for twelve months but after starting a new relationship with a young woman who was using ice, he succumbed to the temptation and once again found himself trapped in the cycle of addiction. Over the following few years Aaron's life spiralled out of control, as he found himself again plummeting into the deep, dark pit of the ice world. Twice Aaron was attacked and beaten up by drug dealers he owed money to. On both occasions he ended up badly injured in hospital.

As much as Aaron was deeply loved by his family and friends, tragically his battle finally took its toll. At the age of 22, unable to cope with the demons of addiction and the mess he had got himself into, this precious young man took his own life.

~~~~~~~~~~

Aaron's story - *from the perspective of his loving and devastated Mother…*

It all started one afternoon seven years ago. A phone call from a young girl; a girl I didn't know and still have no idea who she was, says, "Hi, you don't know me but I'm a friend of Aaron's and I'm not sure if you know, but Aaron is really, really bad on the ICE drug."

My heart sank. "What do you mean? Who are you? What are you talking about?" I said.

"I'm sorry," she said. "I'm just worried about him. Worried it's getting out of control. I'm scared for him." She said, "Did you not notice anything different in him?"

"NO! No I did not!" I said. That was the problem. That's what I couldn't understand. Aaron was a normal fifteen year old. He was working and working hard. He would go out but normally came home. He had his days where you could have killed him, just being a normal fifteen year old and he was 'always right and knew everything'. But what you saw on TV about people on drugs. No! That was not my son.

She says, "Aaron got the stuff at work from a married man with a little boy and he is now getting Aaron to sell the stuff for him."

So I fall to the ground. I'm at work and unable to breath. My worst nightmare had just come true. One of my kids was on drugs. "We aren't one of those families." I thought. "We aren't bad people. I believe in God. We are good and we don't do this. We can't have this. Oh God help me. How do I live through this? How did this happen? Oh my God, I'm a really bad Mum.

Why did I not see this? OMG my son is going to die, die to drugs if he doesn't stop."

So as a Mum I knew I had to take this and I had to be strong. I had to try to fight it. I was not going to let it destroy my family; I have two other boys. I kept no secrets from them. They had to know how bad this drug is; any drug not just ice.

I was there for Aaron all of the time. Yes, I gave him money. I know it was wrong, but he was my son and he needed the money and I gave it (you would too, trust me).

We had good days, where there was hope that he'd seen the light. He was stopping. Then there were bad days.

Aaron's girlfriend at the time had twin girls and I thought OMG, this might just be the turning point - but only for a little time did that help, 'cause that devil's drug was stronger than those girls. It's a real bastard!

So I tried everything. Doctors, medicine, rehab, counselling; you name it, we did it. Aaron got into trouble with the law, driving offences, possession of drugs. OMG life was getting worse. He lost his job. He was sleeping a lot, not really caring about much.

"Things were ok," he thought. "We were all going on about nothing. It's not as bad as we were all making out."

Aaron would say, "Mum, it's ok. I'm ok. I'm going to be ok, don't worry."

"When you stop taking that shit love, then I will stop worrying." I would say.

"I will Mum, I promise. I will, just don't worry." He would say.

Aaron's famous words were, "Don't worry Mum."

Aaron's loving mother, who is an incredibly strong woman, wants Aaron's story to serve as a warning to young people who might be tempted to try ice and she has generously given me permission to print his heart-rending suicide note in the hope that others may listen. She also said that it wasn't necessary to withhold Aaron's full name because, in her words,

"This is not our fault. We are a good family. This is a huge problem in this country and people need to know about it."

"19/11/1993 - 13/4/2016
Goodbye <3 Aaron Davis"

"Hi, my name is Aaron Davis,

I am a 22 year old who unfortunately fell down the horrid path of ice addiction.

I have been an ice addict since the age of fifteen. There were six months of rehab but it didn't work because, well I didn't want it to. There was also twelve months after getting busted that I stayed clean, but again the devil pulled me back in...

My mum used to call it the devil and I used to think "If only she knew how good it was and how it made you feel." But guess what? Like always, Mum was right!

Yes, I met some amazing people along the way, but I also met a lot of selfish back-stabbing dogs; which is unfortunate, because deep down they actually are good people, they have just been taken over by this devil and they will do whatever, say whatever and become whatever they have to, just to get some - (ice)

This life (of ice addiction) gives you nothing but takes everything you ever loved, cared for, owned; the lot. It will literally hold you by your ankles and shake you while everything falls out....

To my family and friends, I'm sorry.

Sorry for never listening; for never asking for help or for accepting your help when you offered, but I didn't know how I could help myself so I couldn't see how anybody else could...

I'll miss you all dearly and love you forever.

I'll always be there watching over everybody and if you ever need me, just think of me.

Love Aaron Davis. "

On Wednesday April 13, 2016, tragically, Aaron Davis' body was found hanging from a tree in the bushland of Harkaway, Victoria.

Once again, my heart goes out to Aaron's family, friends and loved ones.

Sadly, this is not an uncommon situation as many families across this nation and across the globe, lose precious loved ones to the wretched torment and deadly grip of drug addiction.

What will it take to help people understand that using drugs is like playing with fire? It is a deadly game of chance!

"Life for our family will never be the same. Our hearts ache every day for our beautiful son and brother and we will miss him forever." BoBo Davis

20
Heroin (& other Opioids)

"Beyond hungers full measure"

Heroin is a central nervous system depressant, which means that it slows down the messages travelling between the brain and the body. It is a drug that is derived from a plant known as the opium poppy and belongs to a group of drugs called 'opioids'.

Heroin can take on many different appearances, textures, and purity levels. It can come in the form of a white, brown or rose grey coloured powder, coarse off-white granules or small pieces of brown rock. The different colours can signify the heroin's purity, the different substances, including toxins, that the heroin was cut with, or a different region where the heroin was created. Being "cut" means the heroin is mixed with other powdered substances. This makes using heroin even more dangerous because the user does not know what is mixed in with the heroin.

Heroin is one of the most addictive drugs in the world. The 2016 World Drug Report[54] estimates that there are currently 17.4 million heroin users across the globe and a massive 33 million opioid (prescription medication) users.

Thousands of people die from heroin overdoses every year. As a central nervous system depressant, heroin can slow down the central nervous system to a fatal degree. Most people die from heroin overdoses when their bodies forget to breathe. Heroin makes the user calm and a little bit sleepy, but if they use too much or a stronger dose, they can fall asleep, and when they're asleep their respiratory drive shuts down. When the respiration or breathing is depressed to the degree that it stops, the heart and brain cease to function and the person dies. When a person overdoses on heroin or any opioid for that matter, without immediate medical intervention, death is imminent.

According to a report in The New York Times - Jan 6, 2017, opioid and heroin use is not only making a resurgence, but has killed more than 33,000 people in the USA in 2015.[55]

---

[54] https://www.unodc.org/doc/wdr2016/WORLD_DRUG_REPORT_2016_web.pdf - UNODC - United Nations Office on Drugs and Crime. 2016

[55] https://www.nytimes.com/2017/01/06/us/opioid-crisis-epidemic.html

By M Scott Brauer & other reporters for The New York Times. - Jan 6, 2017

On a local level, just last week police arrested a man with $60,000 worth of heroin in the car park of a hotel a few suburbs away from where I live. On a global scale, $60,000 may not seem that much, but this was just a local incident with a small time dealer.

Although ice is having a massive impact on this country of Australia, heroin use has never disappeared and in fact in some countries seems to be on the increase again. It certainly is in the USA. Two possible explanations for this would be; firstly, no doubt the drug traffickers compete for customers and work hard to push their products in their aim to make big money (with no concern at all of the impact this has on the users); and secondly, ice addicts often reach the point where their body can't keep going at full-speed, which is what a stimulant drug leads to, so they move on to a depressant drug like heroin (or marijuana or alcohol) in an attempt to get off the ice and a new addiction often follows.

My neighbour who is a paramedic, recently informed me that heroin use is once again on the rise in Australia and she has attended several heroin overdoses in the last few weeks. As a former heroin user, who not only overdosed several times but who has witnessed repeatedly the trail of destruction this drug leaves, I am devastated by this news.

Heroin is a drug that has caused so much chaos and heartache over the years. It has led to the highest number of illicit drug overdoses globally and has torn countless families apart, leaving behind a wake of destruction. As with any addiction, the user's life can deteriorate rapidly and consequently impact all who are close to them.

Another of the great tragedies caused by heroin use (and other substances like ice etc.) is that often addicts who have children are so lost in the grip of this drug that they are not capable of parenting. Their parents, not wanting their grandchildren to be caught up in the welfare system, step up to raise them. This is a shockingly sad phenomenon that is rapidly increasing globally, as seniors who should be winding down and enjoying their later years, become parents again and carry the heavy load of raising their grandchildren, in the place of their drug-addicted sons or daughters.

~~~~~~~~~~

Medicinal Opioids   (Legal Opioids)

Opioids have been used for thousands of years as a means of providing pain relief and can be very effective for this purpose. They can be used for acute pain relief after surgery, injury or trauma, for cancer pain, pain arising from disease and even to suppress a dry cough. Opioids can also be used in anaesthesia, together with a combination of other drugs.

Some opioids such as methadone and buprenorphine are used in low doses to help wean patients off some of the more potent opioids such as heroin.

Medicinal opioids are also derived from the opium poppy. Opium farms in Tasmania, the most southern state of Australia, supply 50% of the world's legal opium. These farms are run under very tight regulations. With the high demand for medicinal opium, trial farms have also been introduced in parts of Victoria.

In contrast to these tight regulations for legal opium, illicit opium, produced for the sole purpose of the supply of heroin (or black market opioids) is grown in abundance in 3rd world countries like Afghanistan, where it is very hard to regulate and control as it is also a key source of income for many local residents.

This can also play a part in the activity termed 'Narco-terrorism':

"The Afghan opium trafficking industry provides much of the funding to terrorist groups and transnational crime organizations and is responsible for the continued corruption of government officials, police officers, and intelligence agents in Afghanistan, Pakistan, Iran, and other nations. Aside from increased corruption and funding of terrorists and criminals, the opium trade creates opium and heroin addicts out of men, women, and children across the globe."[56] - Report by Steven Fantigrossi, Syracuse University.

---

[56] https://surface.syr.edu/cgi/viewcontent.cgi?article=1851&context

In other words, when a person is using the illicit drug heroin, they are also most likely financially supporting terrorist and/or other criminal organisations.

Unfortunately, although the medicinal form of opium was originally intended for good purposes, it can also lead to addiction, overdose and death. In fact the highest level of drug overdose worldwide, involves the misuse of prescription drugs, in particular opioids.

The following article from 'The Melbourne Age' by Esther Han - Monday July 24, 2017 gives a clear indication of the magnitude of this issue…

More Australians are dying from accidental opioid overdoses each year, with prescription painkillers rather than heroin now accounting for two-thirds of the fatalities, latest Australian Bureau of Statistics data shows.

An analysis of finalised ABS data by researchers at the National Drug and Alcohol Research Centre found 68 per cent of the 668 overdose deaths in 2013 were related to pharmaceutical opioids – a far cry from the heroin epidemic of the 1990s when the majority of opioid deaths were caused by illicit drugs[57]

Further increasing the likelihood of addiction, overdose or death, prescription drugs have also made

---

=honors_capstone - Steven Fantigrossi -Syracuse University - Jan 5, 2015

[57] http://www.theage.com.au/national/health/prescription-opioids-are-killing-more-australians-than-heroin-australian-bureau-of-statistics-20170720-gxf5wa.html Esther Han - The Age Victoria - July 24, 2017

their way onto the black market and are in high demand by those addicted to them.

Regarding opiates in general, I would hope that my own personal catastrophic story relating to heroin use by myself, my former husband and the people I once knew (who lost their lives to overdose), would serve as a good warning to others. We are just a few of the millions of people around the world, whose lives have been devastated by heroin use and addiction.

21

MDMA - Ecstasy

"In a place, an empty space"

MDMA (3,4-methylenedioxy-methamphetamine) or Ecstasy is a synthetic drug that is often seen as the original 'designer' drug because of its high profile links to the dance music culture in the late 80's and early 90's and it has continued to be widely used ever since.

Ecstasy has both a stimulant and hallucinogenic effect and alters mood and perception. Commonly known as 'Molly', "E" or "X", this drug has long been promoted among teens and young adults as the safe drug, but no drug can be classed as safe. Every drug has the potential to cause harm.

One of the problems associated with ecstasy use is the fact that the pills sold often contain other chemicals and very little MDMA, or even none at all. Sometimes they can contain substances such as synthetic cathinones ('bath salts') or PMA, (Paramethoxyamphetamine) which, when taken, can be fatal. According to the Australian Drug Foundation, PMA has similar but more toxic effects than MDMA. It also takes longer to kick in, making it more likely for users to overdose, and it is being found in ecstasy pills, masquerading as the drug that users think they have paid for.

Professor Steve Allsop from Curtin University said: "Somebody may have taken a particular form of ecstasy last week and felt its effects within 45 minutes, then (next time) they take a different formulation, that could have more PMA, that could take longer to take effect. An hour later they'll take another, which is where we risk overdose."

But it must also be noted that pure MDMA on its own can be fatal. In 1995 a beautiful fifteen year old girl from Canberra, Anna Wood, tragically died after taking ecstasy. A few years back, I witnessed Anna's father on a television news report stating that, "Anna's blood test results showed that she had taken only MDMA; no other drugs were in her system." The point is, it's not always the actual dose or whether it has been mixed with other drugs that are necessarily the issue, but rather the reaction the individual user has to it. Anna suffered the side-effect of excessive body overheating and extreme thirst causing her to drink so much water that she died from severe water intoxication after ingesting MDMA (Ecstasy). To add to the tragedy, her friends had believed this to be a safe drug and tried to alleviate her symptoms by giving her more water, unaware of the danger this posed and of the critical state she was in. (Information sourced from the book 'Anna's Story' by Bronwyn Donaghy.)

Again my heart goes out to Anna's family and friends. I'm sure the pain of losing a loved one to a drug related death, regardless of the circumstances, would take a piece of their heart that could never be replaced.

1995 may seem long ago, but in the last few years in this wonderful country of Australia, we have lost ten other young lives where MDMA was indicated in the deaths.

At this point in time these tragic deaths have clearly not served as enough warning, as it appears we are yet to learn the lesson that drugs can kill.

On Wednesday 20th October 2016, tragically Riki Stephens, a healthy young footballer, was taken off life support and died after taking what he thought was ecstasy while on a team 'end of season' celebration on the Gold Coast. According to reports, it turned out that he had taken a mix of MDMA and a synthetic form of LSD known as 'N-BOMe'. Fifteen other people were also admitted to hospital on the Gold Coast after overdosing on what appeared to be the same drug that weekend.[58] We may think, "Well, that's only ten

---

[58] http://www.smh.com.au/national/footballer-riki-stephens-dies-after-gold-coast-drug-overdose-20161020-gs7dz7.html - by Amy Mitchell-Whittington - October 21, 2016

people who have died," but try telling that to the families and loved ones of any of these young people. They have lost a son, daughter, partner, parent or friend who is gone forever and with them, all of their hopes, dreams and potential. These families will never be the same. The loss of a family member to a drug overdose, which is one of the most pointless deaths possible, is devastating. My heart aches for each of these families.

And again as I am writing, yet another tragic incident involving MDMA (ecstasy) has taken place in Melbourne:

"Three people have died and more than 20 were taken to hospital in Melbourne over the weekend due to suspected overdoses of the drug MDMA, police have told the Melbourne Magistrates Court." - ABC News - 16/01/2017 [59]

As my fingers tap lightly across the keyboard with the details of these reports, all I can say is that the heaviness of my heart is ever increasing as my mind tries to comprehend the weight of grief the families of these young people must be carrying.

*** See Appendix for more reports on MDMA (Ecstasy)

---

[59] http://www.abc.net.au/news/2017-01-16/three-people-die-from-drug-overdoses-in-melbourne/8185134 - by Stephanie Anderson Updated January 16, 2017

22
GHB & Ketamine

"Am I, you, we living a pretence"

GHB or Gammahydroxybuterate commonly known as 'Juice' or 'G', is a very potent central nervous system depressant drug that slows down the messages between the brain and the body. GHB is a naturally occurring neurotransmitter. In 1960 a synthetic form of GHB was developed by a French surgeon, Henri Laborit, as an anaesthetic for use prior to medical procedures. It was also trialled for pain relief.

"In medical studies, GHB was eventually found to be ineffective as a pain-relieving medication and shown to be potentially unsafe for administration after many test subjects experienced seizures, intense bouts of vomiting, and severe swings between consciousness and unconsciousness. If someone has overdosed on GHB, they are at risk of severe respiratory depression or arrest, aspiration of gastric contents (i.e., choking on

their own vomit), falling into a coma, and even death. Due to the likelihood that someone who overdoses on GHB will become unconscious and remain so for several hours, it may be difficult to assess them for the symptoms listed above." [60]

Despite these findings and rather frighteningly, GHB has since been hijacked by criminals and is sold, particularly in the night club scene, as a party drug. GHB usually comes in a colourless liquid form and is sold in small bottles or vials but occasionally comes in a bright blue colour or white powder and less commonly in crystal form. GHB is a drug that carries an extremely high risk of overdose as there is a very fine line between the amount a person needs to take to get 'high' and the amount it takes to overdose. The difference is about 1 ml. It is also reported to be one of the most commonly used 'date rape' drugs as in its clear, odourless liquid form, it can easily be slipped into a drink.

The danger of using GHB is greatly multiplied when mixed with either alcohol or any other drugs. On Monday April 11, 2011 The Melbourne Herald Sun had a front page report stating that we have "9000 Overdoses a Year in our City". The image with the article was of an unconscious young man who had

---

[60] http://www.projectknow.com/research/ghb-overdose/ - by Cassandra Keuma, MA Project Know

reportedly overdosed on GHB, and who (also according to the report) had been very lucky to survive. Although GHB overdose is very common, the figures reported in this article took into account all drug overdoses including every other drug used across this city. I personally contacted Ambulance Victoria and discovered that the actual figure is far higher than 9000, as they combined poisonings with drug overdoses. Regardless, this is a very disturbing situation.

The interesting thing is that this figure does not include the overdose of my boyfriend or the overdoses that I suffered or others that I witnessed, as we were extremely fortunate to be able to resuscitate each other, without the need of an ambulance. I mention this to suggest that the reader think deeply about the reality of the risk of drug overdose. Clearly many more people do actually overdose on drugs each year, both illicit and prescription, than what has been recorded. It is alarming to think of just how many people come so close to death as a result of drug use.

On August 27, 2010, it has been reported that AFL footballer Travis Tuck was discovered by police, unconscious in his car, suffering a suspected GHB overdose. This occurred in Berwick, which is not far from where I live and according to the article I read, Travis was very lucky to be found and also very lucky to survive as the paramedics had to work hard to resuscitate him. Tuck is related to several very well-known Australian football players and was selected with a father-son selection in the 2005 AFL Draft. He was one of Hawthorn's numerous developing players, "displaying good football smarts, versatility, and size." According to newspaper reports and sadly for Travis, this was not his first drug offence and he became the first AFL footballer to receive the "Third strike and out" ruling under the Australian Football League's illicit drugs policy. The investigations that followed revealed that Travis had been using drugs as a result of clinical depression.

Tragically, it is not uncommon for people suffering from depression to attempt to 'self-medicate'. Depression can be a serious mental health issue and if ongoing, must be addressed and treated by a health professional. Self-medicating so often has disastrous outcomes.

The good news is that not only did Travis survive, but he is now "getting his life back together." [61] [62] [63]

AND AGAIN right at this moment as I write, yet another devastating incident is reported to have occurred in Melbourne:

---

[61] https://en.wikipedia.org/wiki/Travis_Tuck - Wikipedia
[62] http://www.adelaidenow.com.au/sport/afl/former-hawk-travis-tuck-puts-his-life-back-together-with-bloods/news-story/b33072b825816c26b1590c72d1900bb3 - by Jai Bednall, July 26, 2013
[63] http://www.abc.net.au/am/content/2010/s2998023.htm - by Kellie Lazzaro -August 31, 2010

"More than 20 people were hospitalised and 40 arrested at the Electric Parade dance music festival at the Sidney Myer Music Bowl on Saturday night." - The Age, February 19, 2017.

"It is believed they had overdosed on the synthetic drug GHB."[64]

This was labelled as "One of Melbourne's worst mass overdoses" despite a similar incident happening at the same dance party in 2016.

To make this even more tragic, many drug users never think that they will die, even after experiencing a serious overdose. It only happens to other people. This was certainly the case with me. Drug use has a way of blinding users to reality. However, today with a clear head, I can see just how close some of my own past incidents were to being fatal. The slightest memory of this sends a chill down my spine.

The number of GHB ambulance attendances in 2013/14 increased by 7.4% (up to 626 attendances) in metropolitan Melbourne and 3% (59) in regional Victoria from the previous year. - See more at: http://www.druginfo.adf.org.au/topics/quick-statistics#GHB

~~~~~~~~~~

---

[64] *http://www.theage.com.au/victoria/more-than-20-drug-overdoses-at-electric-parade-dance-party- 20170218-gug5as.html* Neelima Choahan, Benjamin Millar, Steve Lillebuen Feb 19, 2017

Ketamine is also a central nervous system depressant with dissociative and hallucinogenic effects and is used by medical practitioners and veterinarians as an anaesthetic or for acute pain relief.

Once again criminals have hijacked a potent drug that is supposed to be used for legal medicinal purposes only and they are pushing it on the streets and in night clubs as a recreational drug. When sold illegally, ketamine usually comes as a white crystalline powder. It can also be made into tablets and pills, or dissolved in a liquid.

The symptoms of ketamine overdose can be frightening and can include any or all of the following:

Inability to move, rigid muscles, high body temperature, fast heartbeat, convulsions, coma, 'near death' experiences and death!

Large, repeated doses of ketamine may eventually cause 'ketamine bladder syndrome', a painful condition that requires ongoing treatment. Symptoms include difficulty holding in urine, and incontinence, which can cause ulceration in the bladder. In some cases the bladder can be completely destroyed by ketamine use.

23

New Psychoactive Substances (NPS)

(Synthetic Drugs)

"Covered in the dust of a crooked trail…"

Before I begin to write on this topic I believe it is important to mention the following which was reported on Wednesday March 8, 2017:

Synthetic drugs such as "herbal highs" and "party pills" will be banned in Victoria, Australia as the State Government moves to close a legal loophole. The legislation will be amended to apply a blanket ban to the production, sale and promotion of any substance that has a psychoactive effect.[65]

With our current knowledge of the dangers of using NPS, several other nations have also outlawed

---

[65] http://mobile.abc.net.au/news/2017-03-08/all-synthetic-drug.s-to-be-outlawed-in-victoria/8334958 by James Hancock - March 8, 2017

Psychoactive Substances making it illegal to produce, supply, or import them in any form for human consumption.

The term "new" does not necessarily refer to new inventions as several NPS were first synthesized 40 years ago. Rather it refers to substances that have recently become available on the market. Almost any chemical substance can be synthesised and as drug manufacturers and dealers are in the business of making money, they will go to any length to achieve this.

New psychoactive substances (NPS) are drugs which were designed to replicate the effects of illegal substances like cannabis, cocaine, LSD and ecstasy etc., whilst remaining legal – hence their previous name 'legal highs'. As mentioned this 'legal' status is about to be changed.

Effects: The effects of NPS vary significantly from drug to drug and, compared to more traditional drugs, we have relatively little information on them. However, there is a growing body of evidence to demonstrate the potential short and long-term harms associated with their use. There have been numerous hospitalisations and deaths reported to be linked to NPS in this country and across the globe. These chemicals can be so potent that they have been reported to render a user brain dead with one 'hit'.[66] [67]

---

[66] http://www.dailymail.co.uk/news/article-2721002/It-poison-Family-share-heartbreaking-photographs-sons-final-moments-

The Scottish Drugs Forum carried out a survey of drug services in 2013 which summarised some of the key reported harms of NPS during intoxication and comedown:

- Overdose and temporary psychotic states and unpredictable behaviours;
- Attendance at A&E and some hospital admissions;
- Sudden increase in body temperature, heart rate, coma and risk to internal organs (PMA);
- Hallucination and vomiting;
- Confusion leading to aggression and violence;
- Intense comedown that can cause users to feel suicidal.

NPS use was also associated with longer term health issues:

- Increase in mental health issues including psychosis, paranoia, anxiety, 'psychiatric complications';
- Depression;

---

hospital-died-taking-ONE-hit-synthetic-marijuana-warn-dangers-drug.html - By A Greg - Aug 11, 2014

[67]http://www.syracuse.com/crime/index.ssf/2017/05/in_24_hours_at_least_15_people_overdosed_on_synthetic_marijuana_in_syracuse.html - by Samantha House and James T. Mulder - Syracuse.com May 25, 2017

- Physical and psychological dependency happening quite rapidly after a relatively short intense period of use (weeks)[68]

~~~~~~~~

"To think these are just legal highs is incorrect, these are dangerous drugs and we need to get them off our streets." - Victoria Police Minister, Lisa Neville

---

[68] http://www.drugwise.org.uk/wp-content/uploads/NPSComeofAge.pdf
- by Harry Shapiro - Drugwise - May 2016

24

Alcohol

"Sometimes too much"

As I begin to write this chapter I am cautiously encouraged by reports in the newspapers and television news broadcasts across the country today.

The Melbourne Herald Sun Newspaper shows an article headed:

"Teens saying 'No' to Booze….. Drinking rates halved."

Herald Sun Friday October 7, 2016 [69] and ABC News. [70]

The article which is quoting figures from the 'Australian Institute of Health and Welfare' data, states

---

[69] http://www.heraldsun.com.au/news/teenagers-reject-aussie-drinking-culture-data-reveals/news-story/ef003fcf9cf57674fcc2d75d7c91515a

[70] http://www.abc.net.au/news/2016-06-29/young-australians-drinking-much-less-than-previous-generations/7553970 - By Patrick Wright - ABC News - June 29, 2016

that the drinking rate among teenagers (14-17) has halved from 56% to just 25% in a decade!

According to the article, some possible contributing factors include: increasing diversity of cultures, some of which are not part of the alcohol drinking culture; fewer parents buying alcohol for their teenage children, as laws have been tightened regarding underage drinking; more young people are living at home for longer with very little financial independence and more teenagers have become aware of the health consequences, including the fact that sport and fitness is really important to them; and possibly even some of the alcohol awareness education is getting through.

On the other hand, it has also been suggested, that perhaps the report is indicating that teens are choosing to use other substances rather than alcohol. Although we know illicit drug use is a big issue, I would like to think and hope that just maybe some teens are actually waking up to the dangers of binge drinking in particular and that this might be the beginning of a change in our teenage drinking culture. Big dream!

However, we are not there yet. Sadly, there will undoubtedly be further disastrous incidents occurring as a result of alcohol use and abuse and although today's news is encouraging, it is clearly still necessary to cover some of the relevant information regarding the dangers posed by drinking excessive amounts of alcohol.

~~~~~~~~~

Alcohol is also classed as a drug and it is a very potent drug. It is a depressant drug, which means that it slows down the messages between the brain and the body. The fact that alcohol is legal in no way indicates that it is harmless. It is reported that alcohol actually destroys more lives in this country than any other single drug.

In fact in 2014 the World Health Organisation reported that **Alcohol KILLS one person every ten seconds world-wide.**[71] According to the figures listed below, that indicates that fifteen of them will be Australians.

According to FARE, it is estimated that the annual social cost for Alcohol addiction in Australia is $36 Billion:

Alcohol

The Foundation for Alcohol Research and Education (FARE) is an independent, not-for-profit organisation working to stop the harm caused by alcohol.

Alcohol harm in Australia is significant. More than 5,500 lives are lost every year and more than 157,000 people hospitalised, making alcohol one of our nation's greatest preventive health challenges. The devastation

---

[71] http://time.com/96082/alcohol-consumption-who/ - Alexandra Sifferlin - TIME Health - May 12, 2014

doesn't stop there; the high personal and financial toll extends well beyond the individual drinker. Each year nearly 400 people die, and 70,000 Australians are victims of alcohol-related assaults, including 24,000 victims of alcohol-related domestic violence. All these harms cost the nation an estimated $36 billion annually.[72]

The $36 Billion :

- $6.39 billion - Pain and suffering from diminished quality of life;
- $9,300 million - Cost of time lost or spent;
- $4,621 million - Loss of life;
- $3,954 million - Labour costs;
- $2,576 million - Out-of-pocket expenses;
- $2,461 million - Road accidents;
- $2,210 million - Total health care;
- $1,888 million - Resources used in abusive consumption;
- $1,592 million – Crime;
- $670 million - Child protection costs; and
- $396 million - Pain and suffering.

---

[72]http://www.fare.org.au/wp-content/uploads/research/36-Billion.pdf - by D.J. Collins and H.M. Lapsley, The Costs of Tobacco, Alcohol and Illicit Drug Abuse to Australian Society in 2004/05 - FARE - 2008

Binge Drinking Can Kill

Binge drinking is described as the practice of consuming large quantities of alcohol in a single session, usually defined as five or more drinks at one time for a man, or four or more drinks at one time for a woman. Binge drinking can cause blackouts, memory loss and anxiety, and as a consequence can affect a person's judgement and control. Long-term drinking can result in permanent brain damage, serious mental health problems and alcohol dependence or alcoholism. Young people's brains are particularly vulnerable because the brain is still developing. Alcohol can permanently damage parts of the brain, affecting behaviour, memory and the ability to learn.

A few years back, a friend who is an Intensive Care Nurse in a local hospital told me the following:

"Young people who have been binge drinking can suffer from what is called 'alcohol poisoning' and this can be so severe that the patient can go into heart failure and die. The condition is called Ventricular Fibrillation and can be caused by drinking just alcohol on its own, particularly spirits, with no other drugs indicated."

~ ~ ~ ~ ~ ~ ~ ~ ~ ~

- On average, there were 34 alcohol-related ambulance attendances in metropolitan Melbourne per day in 2013/14 (11% increase from 2011/12), and 11 per day in regional Victoria

(8% increase). The average age of these patients was forty years.

(This average age of forty years should serve as a warning to young drinkers as it clearly indicates that early drinking can lead to a life-long battle with alcohol addiction)

- Alcohol was reported to be the reason for the majority of drug-related ambulance attendances, with 12,482 attendances in 2013/14 compared to 3,021 for benzodiazepines, 1,869 for heroin, 1,714 for non-opioid analgesics (such as paracetamol) and 1,237 for crystal methamphetamine (ice).
- See more on alcohol harms at: www.adf.org.au click on drug facts and then on alcohol.

Alcohol is also considered to be a carcinogen and can lead to several types of cancer

The National Cancer Institute states:

"Based on extensive reviews of research studies, there is a strong scientific consensus of an association between alcohol drinking and several types of cancer. Clear patterns have emerged between alcohol consumption and the development of the following types of cancer: head and neck cancer; oesophageal cancer; liver cancer; breast cancer and colorectal cancer.[73] In fact alcohol has been identified by the International Agency for Research on Cancer (IARC) as a Class 1 carcinogen and labels with detailed warnings about cancer risks are being considered for alcohol products."[74]

In Australia there is also another shocking alcohol related issue which was touched on earlier. Alcohol is involved in up to two of every three domestic violence incidents and as many as half of all child-protection cases, depending on the state or territory.[75] This is yet another devastating consequence of alcohol abuse affecting families across this nation and across the globe.

And of course the other well-known side-effect of alcohol use is its contribution to the national road toll.

As I have touched on earlier, I have some dear friends who have lost loved ones to alcohol and other drug related road accidents. One very close friend's precious seventeen year old son lost his life in a tragic incident a few years ago. He and another friend, who had been upset by a particular situation, had been

---

[73] https://www.cancer.gov/about-cancer/causes-prevention/risk/alcohol/alcohol-fact-sheet   NIH The website of the National Cancer Institute (https://www.cancer.gov) Reviewed Jun 24, 2013
[74] https://www.ncbi.nlm.nih.gov/pmc/articles/PMC4750299/ - by Emma R. Miller, ⊠ Imogen J. Ramsey, Genevieve Y. Baratiny, and Ian N. Olver - - PMC - February 11, 2016
[75] http://www.dailyadvertiser.com.au/story/2915888/alcohol-abuse-is-no-stranger-to-us/ - by Ray Goodlass July 25, 2017

drinking alcohol and smoking marijuana. My friend's son was trying to calm his distressed friend by giving him more marijuana thinking he might sleep, but instead the friend insisted on getting into the car and together they drove off never to return. The driver, who knew the road well, totally missed a bend and went head first into the bank of a creek where they were both killed instantly. The repercussions of that tragic night affected not only those who were involved, but sons, friends, mothers, wives, girlfriends, sisters, brothers and the grief also led to loss of jobs, depression and trauma that is still being felt today. Tragically, families across the globe are faced with this shocking and devastating news far too often.

To attend this popular young man's funeral and witness his best friends and family standing at the front of the chapel, with arms around each other in mutual support, as they tearfully shared stories of him and how much he meant to them, was heart rending. This destruction of life is totally avoidable.

This is an event that occurs on a daily basis across the cities and towns of this beautiful nation and right around the world. Families are left shattered as they try to adjust to life without an irreplaceable loved one after losing them to such a shocking and pointless incident.

Although people in all age groups lose their lives in this manner, tragically the highest percentage of road related deaths in this nation is in the 17 - 25 year age group. This reportedly makes up 40% of all road deaths in Australia. What a waste of young lives.

To anyone reading this; I'd like to remind you, you are not indestructible. This can happen to anyone and when alcohol or drugs are involved the chance of injury or death is greatly increased. If you are going to a party or any social event and you expect to drink alcohol, have a plan.

Firstly, don't ever get in the driver's seat of a car while under the influence of drugs or alcohol.

Secondly, if you are going out with friends, have a designated driver; someone who is committed to not drinking or using any substances and also committed to driving their friends home safely.

Thirdly, if you have planned to be a passenger of a vehicle where the driver has been drinking or using drugs, don't get in the car! If possible take the keys from the driver and do your best to convince them not to drive. Another good plan if possible, is to make sure that your parents are available to pick you up or even pay for a cab if necessary, in order to get you safely home. Or even make a plan to stay the night.

We are losing far too many young people needlessly on our roads as a result of drink and/or drug driving; young people, who are robbed of a future and whose loss can traumatise loved ones, leaving a hole in their heart and their life that, can never be filled. And to add to that there are the innocent people in passenger seats or in other cars that are also involved in the incident who may be injured or killed. Tragically, often it is their best friends or relatives who are killed while travelling in the car they are driving.

Then of course there are the legal repercussions. People who drive while under the influence of drugs or alcohol and cause an accident leading to death, often face years of imprisonment. As if that's not enough, along with the punishment, they also have the heavy weight of guilt and regret to carry for the rest of their lives.

Please pause for a moment and think about this.

25
What to do in an Emergency!!!

Unfortunately sometimes plans to have a fun night out can turn to disaster as alcohol and other drug use can lead to overdose or a severe adverse reaction. No level of drug use should be considered safe. The following is a simple list of actions to take in case of an emergency.

    Firstly, always know the exact address of the party or function you plan to attend.

    Secondly, if you ever find yourself in a situation where you are out with friends, either at a party or club etc., and one of your friends or anyone else for that matter, begins to show signs of drug or alcohol related distress or overdose including :

. loss of consciousness
. slipping in and out of consciousness
. seizures/convulsions
. vomiting uncontrollably

. racing heart
. behaving erratically or freaking out
. total confusion

Or any behaviour that is out of character and concerning…

Dial 000

- Call an Ambulance. The operator will ask if you want Police, Fire Brigade or Ambulance.
- Say "Ambulance."
- Stay with the patient. If possible, turn them onto their side into the recovery position, so they will not vomit and choke on their vomit.
- If possible find out what substances the patient has taken.
- Appoint a second person to go to the road to meet the ambulance, so the paramedics can be quickly directed to the patient.
- Stay on the line to the operator. Ambulance operators are highly trained to calmly talk you through the situation. They will ask questions about the patient. Answer the questions clearly and follow the operator's instructions.
- At this point an ambulance has already been dispatched so don't get stressed about the operators continued questions. They need as

much information as possible to assist the paramedics with treatment for the patient.
- Do not give the patient ANYTHING to eat or drink, unless instructed by the operator.
- Stay with the patient while on the line to the operator, until the ambulance arrives.
- Do not worry about the possibility of the police becoming involved. The ambulance operator is under no obligation to call police. They do not want anyone to be too afraid to call an ambulance. Their primary concern is for the patient. Police are only called if there is any violence involved, putting the paramedics at risk.
- Do not worry about whether or not the patient has ambulance cover. You have to weigh up the value of a life and the difference between calling an ambulance and potentially saving a life, or possibly not calling and the chance of a life being lost.

**NOTE:

There is a free phone App available across Australia that can be downloaded onto a mobile phone called '**EMERGENCY+**'. (Other countries may have a similar app.)

When opened, the 'Emergency+' App gives you the option of dialling 000 for Police, Ambulance or Fire brigade, or SES (State Emergency Service).

This is a GPS App and will give the exact GPS coordinates of your position and also the actual address of your location. You can use this to tell the operator your location.

If you are thinking that this could never happen to you, just as a reminder, perhaps a Google search into the number of celebrities and sportspeople, who have tragically had drugs or alcohol implicated in their passing, might give some further perspective into the potential deadly danger of alcohol and other drug use.

26

Who Benefits?

"At truth's expense"

While this topic may be a bit controversial, it's actually pretty obvious. The big question is; who benefits?

Who is it that profits the most from the sale of alcohol and other drugs?

Where alcohol is concerned, clearly it would have to be the liquor companies and distributors. The annual turnover for alcohol sales in this country is in the $Billions.

In the case of illicit drug use, obviously it's the drug dealers and traffickers who gain the most profit.

And to use another example when cigarettes are sold, it is the tobacco companies and distributors who benefit most. And so it goes on.

Of course many may think that it is the government that benefits most as they take a high percentage of tax from alcohol and cigarette sales. However, according to data, the cost of picking up the pieces caused by the side-effects of these addictive substances far outweighs the benefit of the taxes. I guess you could say that the taxes need to be applied to clean up the aftermath of cigarette and alcohol addiction. (See list compiled by F.A.R.E in Chapter 24). Naturally, no taxes are taken from the sale of illicit drugs and yet the social cost is enormous, adding to the financial burden on the government.

The distribution of all of these products is big business! Those producing and selling these products are purely motivated by making money. (Two of these products are legal and one illegal). Yes, they want our money. Despite the myriads of research results, reports and hospital emergency room statistics, indicating the devastating and often deadly consequences of using each of these products, they are continually promoted and pushed on us mere human beings.

And the most troubling point is that much of this marketing, legal or illicit, is aimed at our youth. The big problem with this is that the immature brain of a young person is very impressionable, more easily rewired and consequently more susceptible to addiction. In other words, the earlier a person begins to drink alcohol, smoke cigarettes or use drugs etc., the more likely they are to become addicted.

Sadly the next logical conclusion is - this is exactly who the distributor makes most of their money from;

the person with an addiction and much of the marketing for these products is aimed at people under the age of thirty, in other words, those with an immature brain.

For example, if I was to buy one bottle of wine per year, no one would really make any profit from me. However, if I was to drink one or two bottles of wine a night or perhaps a slab of beer a night, then the liquor companies would do well from my drinking.

The same goes for cigarettes. Today we know only too well the devastating side effects of cigarette smoking, but over the years the combination of the reduction of cigarette advertising, legal smoking areas and the increase of anti-smoking campaigns has reportedly reduced the number of smokers. However, many young people are still falling into this deadly trap and the cigarette companies continue to profit. If they weren't making good money, they would close down.

For the illicit drug dealers and traffickers, this is big business. In fact the illicit drug trade is reported to be one of the largest industries in the world. It's right up there with food, oil, illegal weapons trade and human trafficking. So beginning with the big-time traffickers, right down to the little local dealer, all they want is our money. They have no regard for our health, our welfare, our families or our future. It is all about money. $$$$$

This is a fact I sincerely hope the reader will take note of.

Another important issue to think about is that when we do use illicit drugs, we are supporting criminal activity. We are lining the pockets of the very people who not only want our money, but whose conduct leads to so much trauma and grief in the lives of those who become addicted.

*** NOTE: When using the example of alcohol, I am not talking about responsible drinking. I am not trying to disrespect responsible alcohol drinkers, who may have the occasional drink, but rather I am referring to the issue of binge drinking, heavy drinking and alcoholism.

*** For a more comprehensive list of alcohol and other drugs, their effects, the risks and overdose symptoms, please go to the Australian Drug Foundation site at:

www.druginfo.adf.org.au

- Alcohol and Drug Foundation

27

Why Drugs or Alcohol?

"The answer searching the altitude of latitude"

So why do young people, or older people for that matter, use drugs and alcohol? While there are many different reasons for substance use, in summary I would have to say that the majority of people who use drugs and alcohol come under a few main categories.

As human beings we tend to be social by nature. So firstly there are those who just want to fit in. Fitting in with a group of friends, somehow fills part of a deep need we all have to belong, and an element of belonging includes sharing experiences.

Next they follow their friends into the party scene where alcohol and drug use is rife. With people all around them using both drugs and alcohol it can be so easy to join in without really thinking about the possible consequences. It just looks like a bit of fun and unfortunately, it's also perceived to be cool. But don't start me on that one! The behaviour of people heavily affected by substances can be so 'un-cool' (I sure know about that) and at times downright dangerous.

Sometimes, particularly regarding illicit drugs, it can be peer pressure where friends will say something like, "Come on, just give it a go;" or "Don't be a wuss;" or even, "This is amazing, you'll love it." They might even tell you, "Don't listen to the media; this 'stuff' is harmless." And for some this may be true. It's a fact that not everyone who uses drugs or alcohol ends up dead or totally destroying their lives, but many do. Just ask the families who have suffered the effects of having a loved one battling drug or alcohol addiction. This is a huge 'game' of chance. Then of course sometimes drug users' simply want their friends to join them so that they're not using drugs alone. Whatever the case, it can be all too easy to cross that seemingly innocent line into the world of drug and alcohol use and abuse.

However, probably most commonly teens simply put pressure on themselves and, even though they are not necessarily pushed by anyone else, they feel that in order to fit in or to be part of the group, they should join in. In fact friends often actually warn others about the dangers, particularly regarding drugs, probably not wanting to be the one who opened the door for them. And then of course curiosity and just the desire to have fun can also play a big part. This scenario was pretty much the case for me, I didn't want to be left out and not much has changed. As human beings, we do have somewhat of a herd mentality and like sheep, we can be easily led.

However, it is important to note that that not everyone is this easily led. Many young people DO hear the warning bells and make the decision not to cross that line. This can be tough to do though, as they can be treated as different or outside of the group. They can even be called names like 'losers' or 'killjoys', etc. (which is a form of bullying). Let me tell you from someone who has been there, it takes a lot of courage in a group situation to stand up and say that you don't want to join in. However, I clearly recall having a lot of respect for those who stood their ground!

I realise there are also people who believe we should be free to put whatever we like into our own bodies. And I get that opinion. But I would guess that those who feel this way have most likely not experienced the trauma of a severe, life-controlling addiction or the loss of a loved one to drugs or alcohol; let alone truly considered the overall effect and cost of substance abuse on society.

Then there is the second and sadly, all too common category of drug and alcohol users:

Many of us grow up in safe, secure, loving homes but some of us do not. We live in a very complex society with countless individuals affected by traumas of all kinds, ranging from broken families to grief or even mental, emotional, physical or sexual abuse etc.

*** See Appendix for some trauma related information from within Australia.

Human beings can be incredibly fragile mentally and emotionally and often people who are affected by a traumatic event or situation, find they can't cope with the trauma and turn to alcohol or other drugs to self-medicate in an attempt to 'numb' the pain. I have seen this time and again. Believe me, drugs and alcohol are not the answer. If a person has a problem and they use un-prescribed drugs or alcohol to try to cope with the pain, then they have two problems. Attempting to block out emotional pain in this way only complicates the situation and sadly, addiction often follows.

Thirdly and also very sadly, numerous people worldwide suffer from different forms of mental illness; for example, depression or anxiety and even schizophrenia or personality disorders etc. It is well known among the medical profession that people with one or more of these diagnoses, often self-medicate in an attempt to mask or ease the symptoms and in the process can become addicted to the substance they are using.

We know that the taking of any mind altering substance can lead to mental health issues in people with no prior diagnosed condition. So for those who have a pre-existing mental health diagnosis, self-medicating with any of these substances carries even greater risks of further mental health complications. When a person suffers from both a diagnosed mental illness and drug or alcohol abuse it is classed as a 'dual diagnosis'.[76]

And fourthly, as mentioned earlier, tragically people who have been prescribed medication to ease pain following surgery or an injury, can also become addicted to the very drugs they have been given to help them. Pain-killing medications can change the dopamine levels in the brain in the same manner that illicit drugs can. Likewise, medications prescribed to ease mental health issues or insomnia can lead to addiction. Extreme care needs to be taken by patients who have been prescribed any of these drugs, particularly regarding opioid or benzodiazepine medications.

However, human beings can also be very resilient and there are many people who don't head down this destructive path in search of healing. In some cases people can become determined not to let a trauma or illness 'win' and they become stronger as a result of this. There have been numerous stories over the years of people who have endured shocking trauma, and yet with the right help, they have overcome their darkest times and gone on to do amazing things with their lives.

The following story is a great example of this.

---

[76] *Dual diagnosis refers to one or more diagnosed mental health problems occurring at the same time as problematic drug and alcohol use, and requires specialised services to deal with both issues.*
https://www2.health.vic.gov.au/mental-health/practice-and-service-quality/specialist-responses/dual-diagnosis

The True Story of Antwone Fisher. - The Power of Encouragement & Hope

Antwone Fisher was born in a prison in the USA. His father had died two months earlier. As a result he grew up as a ward of the state. For over thirteen years he was raised by a couple who abused him horribly. Daily he was beaten down physically, verbally and psychologically. He never received a Christmas gift, birthday gift or even a 'dime' of allowance from his foster parents. For years he was also the victim of sexual abuse.

In school he had lost any natural love for learning and at home was constantly told by his foster mother that he was the worst child in the world. Life for him seemed hopeless. As a result of Antwone's shocking home situation, he had become terribly shy and had developed a stutter. But then something wonderful happened. One day his grade five teacher asked him to read a difficult passage out aloud to his class. This time instead of panicking, he read well, including successfully pronouncing a difficult word.

His teacher, Miss Profit, then did something that changed the direction of his life forever. She praised him. Antwone had become so starved of love and encouragement that he said, "Her words were like lightning bolts and thunderclaps" as he realised that he could do something to better himself.

I'm sure he would have also had some counselling along the way, and amazingly, rather than destroy his life; Antwone Fisher went on to become a successful Hollywood screenwriter. He also married and became a loving father to his daughter; giving her a love that he had never experienced himself.

Antwone made the point that he did not follow the path of his older foster brother and friends into a life of drugs and crime, something he could so easily have done. He made a choice to rise above his appalling circumstances and make the most of his life. (paraphrased)

Source - "Encouragement Changes Everything" by John C. Maxwell

I think the following quote captures Antwone Fisher's story perfectly:

"Hardships often prepare ordinary people for extraordinary destiny."

C.S. Lewis

Unfortunately not everyone has the natural capacity to deal with trauma. As individuals, we are all different and of course that means we all handle situations differently. But there is always hope!

The good news is there is help available. We now live in a society where in general, we have come to understand the effect that trauma, abuse or stress can have on individuals.

Beginning in schools; we have welfare teams, psychologists or chaplains who are freely available to all students to turn to in times of stress of any kind.

There are also numerous organisations that offer 24 hour counselling services or have data bases linked to a myriad of other help services for people of all ages.

In Australia we have [77] Kids Help Line, Beyond Blue Youth, Headspace and Direct Line just to mention a few.

And for those over the age of 25 we have Lifeline, Beyond Blue and many more…

If you are reading this now and you have never been through a tough time in your life, trust me, you will. That is life. Life is a journey of highs and lows. Most of us will have some amazing times throughout our lives, but all of us will also have some times that are not so easy.

Some of us will have more trials, traumas and heartache than we have good times. If there's one thing I've learned over the years it would be this; Never Give Up. If you are going through a difficult time, hang in there. Remind yourself that this will not last. It is actually during the toughest trials in life that we can learn the most lessons; we grow the most as a person.

All of us have some sad or difficult times in our lives and feeling a bit low or a little depressed from time to time is quite normal; particularly after a loss or

---

[77] Help Service contact list at end of book

disappointment or a broken relationship etc. However, if anyone reading this now is facing a trauma that you just can't deal with; if you can't sleep, can't think, if you just can't pick yourself up or if you're crying a lot, for some reason or for no particular reason, or having very negative thoughts, GET SOME HELP! Depression and anxiety are very real and require attention or treatment of some kind. When a person who is really struggling mentally or emotionally, reaches out for help, the right counsellor can help them process their thoughts and emotions and assist them to get their life back on track. (Sometimes it may take a few sessions to see if you have connected with the right person for you, but keep trying.)

*** *Note: When I talk about using substances to deal with mental or emotional pain, I am referring to the dangers of self-medicating. This does not include people who seek professional help and who may be prescribed medication by their health professional to help them through a difficult time.*

If you see a doctor who prescribes some form of medication to alleviate stress, depression or anxiety, you should follow your doctor's instructions carefully. Sometimes this is just a temporary measure to help you through a particularly tough time and as you process the situation with a good counsellor, you may be able to move on from taking medication. But I stress, listen to your health professional. DO NOT self-medicate and likewise, DO NOT stop taking prescribed medication without your health professional's advice.

Look out for each other. This is a crazy world we live in, and one of the best remedies for any emotional or mental strain we may face, is friendship. A listening ear and a gentle, kind word can heal the soul. Be that friend. Don't get involved in gossip or bullying, this is so destructive and tragically, has precipitated many suicides. Bullying is not the behaviour of a normal well-adjusted person. Often bullies have deep issues of their own and rather than seek help, they take their frustration out on others. Treat others the way you would want to be treated. Include people, especially those who appear to be lonely. Respect others, regardless of any differences. If we all considered other people's needs as much as we do our own, this world would be a far better place.

~~~~~~~~~~

I have had the amazing opportunity of speaking in a prison on two occasions and let me tell you many people in there look just like you and me. Sadly, countless people in prisons are there because they have been through some kind of trauma and rather than seek help for that, they have self-medicated with illicit drugs or alcohol in an attempt to numb the pain. Unfortunately for many of these people, addiction follows and they can become caught up in various crimes to support their addiction and as a consequence end up incarcerated.

Of course this does not include everyone in prison; some people just make bad choices. But for those who have been used, abused, or traumatised in life, this is a tragic situation. Had they found the right help at the right time, they may just have prevented this outcome.

"Life is amazing. And then it's awful. And then it's amazing again. And in between the amazing and the awful it's ordinary and mundane and routine. Breathe in the amazing, hold on through the awful, and relax and exhale during the ordinary. That's just living heartbreaking, soul-healing, amazing, awful, ordinary life. And it's breathtakingly beautiful."

L R Knost

28

I Am Not My Mistakes

"My soul to retrieve"

I am not my mistakes. I am a woman, a mother, a daughter, a friend, an encourager, a worker, a helper and a fragile human being who once made some massive, life-changing mistakes. But that was long ago. I have turned my life around. I have done my best to atone for my past. I have forgiven others and myself and I have been forgiven. For the most part, I am healed.

Likewise David is not his mistakes. He is also a fragile, fallible human being who made some very bad choices years ago and he too has paid the price. After a long, difficult battle, he has also totally turned his life around.

Although we know that not everyone who ever touches drugs or alcohol ends up dead or totally destroying their lives, so many do. As mentioned earlier, it is a deadly game of chance, like 'Russian

Roulette', you never know if you will be the one who will get the bullet. The personal, social and financial cost of drug and/or alcohol use and abuse in this country and globally is massive. The lives of millions of individuals, families and their communities are torn apart by the horror of drug and alcohol addiction on a daily basis. Rehabilitation facilities are bursting at the seams with such long waiting lists that many addicts give up hope of ever overcoming addiction or tragically even die while waiting.

Because of my personal story and the field I work in, I regularly receive calls from desperate parents whose son or daughter is battling addiction and I have connected with several of these people and helped guide some into rehab, with some great outcomes. I am on the ground passionately using my experience to make a difference. I hear their stories and I understand the current reality of drug and alcohol addiction. But this is not always an easy road.

Not only do many people battling addiction have a long wait to enter a rehabilitation facility, but most facilities require the patient to complete a drug or alcohol detox before entering their program. As a consequence of this delay, many addicts are left in a precarious state as doubt and fear set in about the choice they have made to seek help. Addiction can really mess with a person's thinking and logic, and the longer they have to wait, the more their mind can fill with negative thoughts regarding rehabilitation.

Unfortunately, at this point people can 'freak out,' and back away from receiving the help they so badly need.

I also receive regular information and updates on current issues nationally and internationally, regarding alcohol and other drugs and the news is not good. I have attended numerous forums on crime and drugs and the clear message is that this beautiful nation of Australia has a huge problem and a big part of that is because of drug and alcohol use and abuse.

This is the time for a generation to stand up and make a difference; to really think about the possible consequences of its choices. To be individuals, who don't just follow the crowd, but who want to be part of a culture that turns the tide on the 'entitlement' thinking of so many young people. If the current trend doesn't change, I believe that this generation and the next will have a heavy burden to carry; the burden of damaged lives and an even greater national debt brought on by drug and alcohol use and abuse. Please pause again to think about this.

29

Dream

"Like a mighty roar"

I am not in any way looking for sympathy, but in short I must say that I have actually had a pretty tough life. I know many people have had a far more difficult life than me, but for me this has been a direct consequence of the choices I made as a teenager; the choice to use drugs. That choice has affected the whole of my life.

In summary: I followed my friends and I got into drugs, I nearly died as a result, I have been left with scars, one of my children has been mildly affected and my ex-husband battled addiction for 26 years beyond the time that I stopped, until I said "Enough", and brought our marriage to an end.

I just want to say, that as a person who has lived with addiction from both sides; firstly being a drug user and then living with a drug user, and as one who has now lived for over thirty years completely free of addiction, but still carries the physical and emotional scars, my message is; it's just not worth it!

~ ~ ~ ~ ~ ~ ~ ~ ~

Some time ago I looked back and asked myself this question: Why did I head down this path? The answer I came up with was this:

I didn't have a dream or a vision for my future. I had no goal or plan for my life. To have a goal or plan or a dream for the future gives our life hope and purpose. I went to school, I got a job and I partied. Without some kind of plan for the future it can be so easy to just drift in life with no real purpose. Living without a purpose can lead to boredom and boredom is an open invitation for drug or alcohol use and often trouble.

> *"The future belongs to those who believe in the beauty of their dreams."*
>
> *Eleanor Roosevelt*

Have a dream! Aspire to do something great. Look to where your gifts and talents lie and follow that path.

Whether it be; career, travel, sport, music, art, fitness, hobbies, adventure, technology or helping others etc., look towards making a plan for your future. It is never too late. Go to the Jobs Guide and look for careers that really interest you. Whether it is academic or working with your hands as in a trade or even artistic creativity, look toward where your interests and your passions lie and make sure you follow the study courses that line up with the career that suits you. Set yourself personal goals along the way towards achieving this.

"Success is the sum of small efforts, repeated day in and day out."

Robert Collier

Volunteer. There are numerous welfare agencies looking for volunteers. Volunteering to help people in need or even at animal welfare agencies etc., is an awesome way to fulfil the desire that we humans all have, to be contributors, to feel needed and to be valued. And of course sometimes a future career can arise from volunteering.

Very few people leave school and just make it big. We all have to put in the work. By the same token, few students excel in their school work without putting in the study time. Everyone has gifts and talents in some area, but the difference between those who make it and those who don't, is hard work. If we do work hard towards reaching a goal, when we reach that goal, the reward is so much greater. The feeling of achievement and self-satisfaction is so fulfilling.

"Talent is cheaper than table salt. What separates the talented individual from the successful one is a lot of hard work."

Stephen King

However, sometimes we don't succeed, even after a lot of hard work. Don't give up. Have a plan 'B'. I read a quote a while back that said, "If plan 'A' doesn't work, there are 25 more letters in the Alphabet." I don't actually think we need to have 26 plans, but the message is clear, don't give up easily; give it your best and have a back-up plan.

The great news today is that in this nation and many others, there are so many opportunities for people to study a new career at any age, so even if after much effort, a particular path you take doesn't come to pass, there are countless other options. I began my current career after my three children had all grown up. My younger brother had done all manner of work over the years, including being a very talented musician, but in recent years he changed direction and although he's still doing gigs and singing with his band, he completed a totally different course and a new door has opened for him.

Regardless of what we may go through in this life, there is always hope.

Human life is precious. Remember this; no matter what you may feel about yourself; no matter what anyone else may have ever said about you, you are valuable! Your life is important! Never forget that and never give up! Regardless of what we may go through in this life, there is always hope!! The journey of highs and lows on this amazing planet can be incredible. But if we don't have some kind of goal or dream for our lives, it can be so easy to just drift in life and aimlessly fall into meaningless and destructive behaviours like drug and alcohol use and abuse. There is so much more to life than that!

"May you follow your dreams and not the path that so often leads to destruction."

Kerryn Redpath

Finale

In my effort to give balance and perspective to my own personal story and the events depicted, I offered David the opportunity to add some comments from his perspective. He accepted my offer and chose to cover his thoughts in the form of a poem.

I have used several lines from David's poem to begin each chapter, a clear indication of the connection between our stories and of the trauma drug addiction inflicted on us both…

Placebo Town (revisited)

Is ' Love ' just another four letter word …
given a life sentence?
Sometimes too little
Sometimes too much … Such is life.
Is this existence a swirling vortex …
of which I must make sense?
Am I, you, we living a pretence …
at truth's expense?
Are we colour living in contrast?

Chasing After The Wind

Or black and white ... out of focus?
Just a biological blast projected on some
future past?
Am I ' True Blue ' ... me ... we?
Am I well and truly set free ...
and in the presence?
Living within the heart and soul
of Holy mindfulness?
Providence with purpose ...
I am on a promise. The word given,
In name, in deed, and in person.
The one who is faithful and true.
Honestly, apparently, a loving spoonful
of truth ... a divine recipe.
With integrity like a hot shot of espresso coffee.
Am I only decaf ... or just Blend 43?
Having been plucked, roasted & ground
in a place called Placebo Town.
Loving justice, the knowing,
showing mercy... requiring the giving and taking
of the occasional selfie at the
Right & Royal Navel Gazing Academy .
Virtuosity... an unexpected journey.
The answer searching the altitude of latitude,
as all hell... with brakes loose,
and then the heavens descending
Finding a true friend.
Even better, a Saviour...
a brother, with a spare dime,
at the Laundromat of Space and Time.
As the Good Samaritan crosses tribal lines,

Chasing After The Wind

through the headwinds,
at the crossroads,
the wonder of a sign ...
from the One who shadows over a multitude of crime.
Not the rumour of a gossip from the marketplace....
not a trace.
Not the whisper of a sound,
heard through the din...of Placebo Town.
The Taker ... climbing the crater of worldly power, with
his pants on fire,
another master's apprentice
from the golden tower.
Silver tongue preaching to the ' rat race choir ',
as All Star Evangelical guns for hire
strut the catwalk of dog eat dog empire.
Where the trained to heel are
' keeping it real ' ...
whilst cutting a deal.
It's always peak hour on the indiscreet streets ...
the zero ground,
in a place, an empty space,
called Placebo Town.

Where mercy gone missing
Where grace freely taken ...
but not given, by the heirs and graces
of the unforgiving.
Where truer words never are spoken.
Where oppression the weapon,
and deception the poison.
Malicious and religious...
both domestic and foreign.

Chasing After The Wind

Where souls are downtrodden and
broken ...
dwelling in the cellar of Placebo Town
The Seafarer ... seeking truth.
Does all plain sailing make you
... a plain sailor?
Prepare to be boarded and searched,
by the Goodship Captain ...
and the interstellar fellow traveller,
from escalator to service elevator.
With permission, on a mission,
my soul to retrieve ...
Lost in the weave of a wicked web ...
A weave so tight
you'd forget how to breathe.
One stich at a time, crossing a finite line,
as virtue retreats...
in the land of giant deceits,
going down in Placebo Town.

So down and laid low,
past tired and sore,
like a piece of junk mail
shoved under death's door.
I felt the flow of water living ~ uplifting.
Heard the whisper on the wind ~
like a mighty roar.
' Ten Four ', above and beyond ...
and even more.
The Angels., from every angle, in awe
and keeping score.
The Living God commands,

Chasing After The Wind

as death so demands,
honesty in totality !
How can any man, born of a woman, stand?
Before the shadow surrounds you ...
a fear you just can't break through,
look to the Son .. in person,
to the One who is faithful and true.
Kingdom Come !
The Dinki Di, out from the shadow of the sky,
as dark energy switches back to light
and dark matter, with glory, reignites.
The concealed revealed from way on high.
The curtain coming down ...
on a place called Placebo Town.

The pusher pushing for proof ...
Is Life a one shot self-inflicted wound,
eternity bound, down the barrel of a gun?
In a land of bumper sticker opinions,
it seems, everybody's got one.
No truth to be found in Placebo Town.
Chasing a desperate treasure,
beyond hunger's full measure ...
Over black seas, under red skies,
past the last post to the hitching rail ...
Covered in the dust of a crooked trail,
with a past you just can't disguise ...
in word or deed.
In need of that wonder working teflon,
the truly fair dinkum.
When all said and done ...
look to the Son.

Chasing After The Wind

Ashes to diamond
... Kingdom Come!
The believer true ...
Integrity you just can't drill through.
The Environmental Criminal now recycling
every blessed molecule.
Life, for a time, a privilege divine ...
Recreation, revelation, the sensation,
endless~loving ~morning sunshine.
The infinite sublime ...
Rivers and streams to cross.
From valleys deep,
the mountains to climb,
in the shadow of your wing.
Unity in purpose...motivation service,
to the Lord of all things.
As the bell of truth rings,
I've still a way to go, till I get to the sea
... through all the to and fro.
May the road rise and the waters flow.
Hope, faith, love and all that
an unexpected tomorrow can bring ...
as the crow flies,
and the Angels sing.

~ by david redpath

www.deepart-from-me.tumblr.com

PART III
Appendix

How Do Drugs Affect The Brain?

The following is an article on "The science of Drug Abuse and Addiction" taken from the NIH - National Institutes of Health on Drug Abuse :

How do drugs work in the brain to produce pleasure?

Most drugs of abuse directly or indirectly target the brain's reward system by flooding the circuit with dopamine. Dopamine is a neurotransmitter present in regions of the brain that regulate movement, emotion, motivation, and feelings of pleasure. When activated at normal levels, this system rewards our natural behaviours. Overstimulating the system with drugs, however, produces euphoric effects, which strongly reinforce the behaviour of drug use—teaching the user to repeat it.

What happens to your brain if you keep taking drugs?

For the brain, the difference between normal rewards and drug rewards can be described as the difference between someone whispering into your ear and someone shouting into a microphone. Just as we turn down the volume on a radio that is too loud, the brain adjusts to the overwhelming surges in dopamine (and other neurotransmitters) by producing less dopamine or by reducing the number of receptors that can receive signals. As a result, dopamine's impact on the reward circuit of the brain of someone who abuses drugs can become abnormally low, and that person's ability to experience any pleasure is reduced. This is why a person who abuses drugs eventually feels flat, lifeless, and depressed, and is unable to enjoy things that were previously pleasurable. Now, the person needs to keep taking drugs again and again just to try and bring his or her dopamine function back up to normal—which only makes the problem worse, like a vicious cycle. Also, the person will often need to take larger amounts of the drug to produce the familiar dopamine high—an effect known as tolerance.[78]

---

[78] www.drugabuse.gov/publications/drugs-brains-behavior-science-addiction/drugs-brain
- NIH - National Drug Institute on Drug Abuse

MARIJUANA

Overview - World Health Organisation

Cannabis is globally the most commonly used psychoactive substance under international control. In 2013, an estimated 181.8 million people aged 15-64 years used cannabis for nonmedical purposes globally (uncertainty estimates 128.5–232.1 million) (UNODC, 2015). There is an increasing demand for treatment for cannabis use disorders and associated health conditions in high- and middle-income countries, and there has been increased attention to the public health aspects of cannabis use and related disorders in international drug policy dialogues.[79]

From Chapter 13 - Examples of black market marijuana existing despite legalisation etc.:

The following are reports from Colorado where marijuana use has been legalised. This was passed by voters on November 6, 2011 and implemented in January 2014.

1. Thousands of marijuana plants found on forest land in Pueblo County [80]

PUEBLO COUNTY, Colorado. — More than 7,400 marijuana plants were discovered in an illegal grow on

---

[79] http://www.who.int/substance_abuse/publications/cannabis/en/
Authors: World Health Organization

[80] http://kdvr.com/2017/07/03/thousands-of-marijuana-plants-found-on-forest-land-in-pueblo-county/ by Sarah Schuller - July 3, 2017 - Fox 31 Denver

Friday in two separate fields on U.S. Forest Service land near Rye, the Pueblo County Sheriff's Office said. The estimated street value is more than $7 million.

2. ICE (Immigration and Customs Enforcement) aids dismantling marijuana grow operations throughout Colorado:[81]

U.S. Department of Homeland Security - News Release - October 8, 2015

Recent investigations into this crime have charged 32 individuals in federal court

DENVER — Within the last six weeks, U.S. Immigration and Customs Enforcement's (ICE) Homeland Security Investigations (HSI) has worked with federal, state and local law enforcement partners to identify and dismantle a large number of illicit marijuana cultivation sites across Colorado.

3. Five acres of marijuana found in Pike National Forest:

The Gazette - By: Kaitlin Durbin   August 11, 2016 Updated: August 11, 2016 at 7:44 pm

---

[81] https://www.ice.gov/news/releases/ice-aids-dismantling-marijuana-grow-operations-throughout-colorado US Dept. of Homeland Security - October, 8 2015

Local, state and federal agencies shut down an illegal marijuana growing operation in Pike National Forest, Colorado, Thursday.

Agents uncovered the 18,300-plant operation on 5 acres off Rampart Range Road, almost 7 miles outside Woodland Park, according to the U.S. Forest Service, which manages the land.

About 2,000 pounds of infrastructure, including irrigation pipes, camping gear, tarps, trash, chemicals to deter wildlife, and multiple 50-pound bags of fertilizer had been installed, the Forest Service said.

No arrests have been made, the Forest Service said.

~ ~ ~ ~ ~ ~ ~ ~ ~

Even casual use of cannabis alters brain, warn scientists…

The Telegraph - By Rebecca Smith, Medical Editor
16 Apr 2014

Smoking marijuana once or twice a week for a matter of months found to have effects on the brain in sections that govern emotion, motivation and addiction.

Experimenting with cannabis on a casual basis damages the brain, research has found.
It is far from being a "safe" drug and no one under the age of 30 should ever use it, experts said.

People who had only used cannabis once or twice a week for a matter of months were found to have changes in the brain that govern emotion, motivation and addiction.
Researchers from Harvard Medical School in America carried out detailed 3D scans on the brains of students who used cannabis casually and were not addicted and compared them with those who had never used it. Two major sections of the brain were found to be affected.[82]

Casual Marijuana Use Linked to Brain Abnormalities
April 16, 2014 By Marla Paul - Northwestern Now

First study to show effects of small time use; more "joints" equal more damage

CHICAGO --- Young adults who used marijuana only recreationally showed significant abnormalities in two key brain regions that are important in emotion and motivation, scientists report. The study was a collaboration between Northwestern Medicine® and Massachusetts General Hospital/Harvard Medical School.[83]

---

[82] http://www.telegraph.co.uk/news/health/news/10768847/Even-casual-use-of-cannabis-alters-brain-warn-scientists.html - Rebecca Smith, Medical Editor - April 16, 2014
[83] https://news.northwestern.edu/stories/2014/04/casual-marijuana-use-linked-to-brain-abnormalities-in-students - Marla Paul - April 16, 2014

Regular pot habit changes your brain, may even lower your IQ, study says

By Saundra Young and Matthew Stucker, CNN
Updated 1447 GMT (2247 HKT) November 11, 2014

Using marijuana at an early age could have long-term consequences on your brain and it may even lower your IQ, according to a new study in the Proceedings of the National Academy of Sciences.

Researchers found that compared to nonusers, people who smoked marijuana starting as early as age 14 have less brain volume, or gray matter, in the orbitofrontal cortex. *That's the area in the front of your brain that helps you make decisions.*

"The younger the individual started using, the more pronounced the changes," said Dr. Francesca Filbey, the study's *principal investigator and associate professor at the School of Behavioral and Brain Sciences at the University of Texas at Dallas.* "Adolescence is when the brain starts maturing and making itself more adult-like, so any exposure to toxic substances can set the course for how your brain ends up."[84]

---

[84] http://edition.cnn.com/2014/11/10/health/pot-and-your-brain/index.html - By Sandra Young and Matther Stucker, CNN November 11, 2014

Potent Pot: Marijuana Is Stronger Now Than It Was 20 Years Ago

By Agata Blaszczak-Boxe, Contributing Writer | February 8, 2016

Pot is becoming more potent, a new study suggests.

In the study, the researchers looked at more than 38,600 samples of illegal marijuana seized by the U.S. Drug Enforcement Administration over 20 years. They found that the level of THC, or tetrahydrocannabinol — marijuana's main psychoactive ingredient — in the marijuana samples rose from about 4 percent in 1995 to about 12 percent in 2014.
Conversely, the level of CBD, or cannabidiol — an ingredient sometimes touted for its potential health benefits — fell from about 0.28 percent in 2001 to less than 0.15 percent in 2014.

When the researchers looked at the ratio of THC to CBD, they found that marijuana in 1995 had a THC level that was 14 times its CBD level. But in 2014, the THC level was 80 times the CBD level.[85]

Debunking Marijuana Myths For Teens

By: Susan D. Swick, M.D., And Michael S. Jellinek, M.D.   December 22, 2015   - Family Practice News

---

[85] https://www.livescience.com/53644-marijuana-is-stronger-now-than-20-years-ago.html By Agata Blaszczak-Boxe Feb 8, 2016

Myth No. 1: Marijuana is medicine

Although 23 states in the USA allow the legal sale of marijuana for "medicinal purposes," it is important to note that there are currently no Food and Drug Administration–approved indications for medical marijuana.

Myth No. 2: Marijuana is safe

Although there is consensus that moderate marijuana use in adulthood poses only limited health risks (including the known risks of smoking), there is robust evidence that marijuana use during youth (through the early 20s) causes several serious and permanent effects on the developing brain.

Beyond these findings of cognitive deficits, evidence is growing that adolescent marijuana use is associated with several psychiatric illnesses, including depression and anxiety. There is especially strong evidence for a causal link between marijuana use and psychotic illnesses in (genetically) vulnerable young people. Until we have a comprehensive knowledge of the relevant genes, and routinely check every patient's complete genetic profile, it is reasonable to assume that any young person using marijuana is significantly increasing the risk of developing schizophrenia, a chronic and disabling condition.

~ ~ ~ ~ ~ ~ ~ ~ ~

MEDICINAL MARIJUANA

Thorough clinical trials of medicinal cannabis needed:

The following is a report from Andy LaFrate, president of Charas Scientific. On NBC news 23/3/2015 :

"CBD is anecdotally known to control depression, anxiety, and pain. About 200 families with ill children also moved to Colorado to access a strain called Charlotte's Web, which appears to control seizures in some kids.

"It's disturbing to me because there are people out there who think they're giving their kids Charlotte's Web. And you could be giving them no CBD — or even worse, you could be giving them a THC-rich product which might actually increase seizures," LaFrate said. "So, it's pretty scary on the medical side."

~ ~ ~ ~ ~ ~ ~ ~ ~

METHAMPHETAMINES – Ice

Methamphetamine use in Australia tripled in past five years, research shows

By Danuta Kozaki - ABC News -Updated 29 Feb 2016

The number of Australians using the illegal drug methamphetamine — including crystal methamphetamine or ice — has tripled over the past five years, the National Drug and Alcohol Research Centre estimates.

A new study published in the Medical Journal of Australia shows there are 268,000 regular and dependent methamphetamine users in Australia.

One of the study's authors, Sarah Larney, said that five years ago the number of users was about 90,000.

For full story go to the following link:

http://www.abc.net.au/news/2016-02-29/trippling-in-methamphetamine-use-australia-five-years/7207012

The Age - Victoria   - August 23 2016
Ice scourge strikes schools
By Henrietta Cook

"The devastating impact of the drug ice has hit Victorian schools, with agencies fielding calls from desperate principals wanting help.
Students are turning up to class ravaged by ice, or crystal methamphetamine, with some teachers now working in pairs for safety.

Agencies are fielding calls from principals who want help dealing with the drug ice.

Victoria's Youth Drug and Alcohol Advice acting manager Cara Munro Steensma said the service had received calls from schools that were worried about ice use among students."

One of the contributing factors is the fact that Ice is more accessible than other drugs because it was easier to make and source its ingredients:

http://www.theage.com.au/victoria/ice-scourge-strikes-schools-20160823-gqz8bg.html
by Henrietta Cook- The Age Victoria - August 23, 2016

~~~~~~~~~

MDMA - Ecstasy

The following is Conducted by the National Drug and Alcohol Research Centre:

THE HEALTH AND PSYCHOLOGICAL EFFECTS OF "ECSTASY (MDMA) USE"
Louisa Degenhardt and Wayne Hall (editors)

The first reports of deaths in persons who had used 3,4-methylenedioxymethamphetamine (MDMA), commonly known as 'ecstasy', appeared in the scientific literature in the late 1980s. Around this time, the setting in which the drug was used began to change from that of clinical psychotherapy in the 1970s to dance party settings in the 1990s. Since then, numerous scientific papers have delineated the potential harms associated with ecstasy use and have identified ecstasy-related fatalities.

Fatalities have been reported where MDMA is the only substance identified by toxicology tests. However, because of patterns of poly-drug use among ecstasy users and the highly variable content of pills sold as ecstasy, many ecstasy-related fatalities are attributable to multiple drug toxicity.

Hyperthermia (i.e. body temperature above 38 C) is one of the major symptoms of acute ecstasy-related toxicity that can lead to often fatal conditions such as rhabdomyolysis, disseminated intravascular coagulation, renal failure and liver damage. The impairment of temperature regulation among ecstasy users is likely to be a direct effect of MDMA in combination with high ambient temperature, prolonged physical activity and insufficient fluid replacement

Over the four year period 2001-2004, the NCIS identified 112 ecstasy-related deaths in Australia73. In 51 (46%) of these cases, ecstasy was determined to be a 'primary' contributing factor, meaning that it produced the physical harm most closely linked to the cause of death. However, only six (5%) of these deaths identified MDMA as the only drug present, suggesting that other substances may have played a part in the majority of ecstasy-related fatalities in Australia during the time period. Since ecstasy was usually one of a range of drugs detected, other drugs were also classified as a primary contributing factor.

Methylenedioxymethamphetamine (MDMA)-related fatalities in Australia:
Demographics, circumstances, toxicology and major organ pathology - Science Direct.
Sharlene Kayea, Shane Darkea, Johan Dufloub

"MDMA has contributed to a clinically significant number of deaths in Australia. MDMA was a direct cause of death in the majority of cases, although, consistent with previous studies of MDMA and other drug-related fatalities combined drug toxicity was more common than toxicity due to MDMA alone. Nevertheless, MDMA alone was a direct cause of death in over 1 in 5 cases. These findings indicate that MDMA toxicity is itself a primary cause of death and not merely a contributor to risk behaviours that result in death. In a minority of cases, however, MDMA toxicity or intoxication was a causal factor in death due to lethal injury."

MDMA is used among a more heterogeneous population and wider variety of environments
than the traditional image of MDMA as a "dance party drug" would suggest, but that the potential risks associated with the consumption of MDMA, particularly in conjunction with other drugs, are not limited to particular settings or activities of the user. As such, consideration of the morbidity and mortality associated with the use of MDMA should extend to all users and to use in a range of contexts.

Effects of MDMA

Reported Undesirable Effects (up to 1 week post-MMDA, or longer):

- Anxiety
- Restlessness
- Irritability
- Sadness
- Impulsiveness
- Aggression
- Sleep Disturbances
- Lack of appetite
- Thirst
- Reduced interest in and pleasure from sex
- Significant reductions in mental abilities

Potential Adverse Health Effects:

- Nausea
- Chills
- Sweating
- Involuntary jaw clenching and teeth grinding
- Muscle cramping
- Blurred vision
- Marked rise in body temperature (hyperthermia)
- Dehydration
- High Blood Pressure
- Heart failure
- Kidney failure
- Arrhythmia

Symptoms of MDMA Overdose:

- High Blood Pressure
- Faintness
- Panic attacks
- Loss of consciousness
- Seizures

As noted, MDMA is not a benign drug. MDMA can produce a variety of adverse health effects, including nausea, chills, sweating, involuntary teeth clenching, muscle cramping, and blurred vision. MDMA overdose can also occur—the symptoms can include high blood pressure, faintness, panic attacks, and in severe cases, a loss of consciousness and seizures.

Because of its stimulant properties and the environments in which it is often taken, MDMA is associated with vigorous physical activity for extended periods. This can lead to one of the most significant, although rare, acute adverse effects—a marked rise in body temperature (hyperthermia). Treatment of hyperthermia requires prompt medical attention, as it can rapidly lead to muscle breakdown, which can in turn result in kidney failure. In addition, dehydration, hypertension, and heart failure may occur in susceptible individuals. MDMA can also reduce the pumping efficiency of the heart, of particular concern during periods of increased physical activity, further complicating these problems.

MDMA is rapidly absorbed into the human bloodstream, but once in the body, MDMA metabolites interfere with the body's ability to metabolize, or break down, the drug.[8] As a result, additional doses of MDMA can produce unexpectedly high blood levels, which could worsen the cardiovascular and other toxic effects of this drug. MDMA also interferes with the metabolism of other drugs, including some of the adulterants that may be found in MDMA tablets.

In the hours after taking the drug, MDMA produces significant reductions in mental abilities. These changes, particularly those affecting memory, can last for up to a week, and possibly longer in regular users. The fact that MDMA markedly impairs information processing emphasizes the potential dangers of performing complex or skilled activities, such as driving a car, while under the influence of this drug.

The Neurobiology of Ecstasy (MDMA)
MDMA alters brain chemistry by binding to serotonin transporters.

Over the course of a week following moderate use of the drug, many MDMA users report feeling a range of emotions, including anxiety, restlessness, irritability, and sadness that in some individuals can be as severe as true clinical depression. Similarly, elevated anxiety, impulsiveness, and aggression, as well as sleep disturbances and lack of appetite have been observed in regular MDMA users. Some of these disturbances may not be directly attributable to MDMA, but may be related to some of the other drugs often used in combination with MDMA, such as cocaine or marijuana, or to adulterants commonly found in MDMA tablets.

https://www.drugabuse.gov/publications/research-reports/mdma-ecstasy-abuse/what-are-effects-mdma - NIH

~~~~~~~~~~

TRAUMA - (Help services list on pg 268)

Information on some of the emotional trauma that can lead to self-medicating with drugs or alcohol:

. Divorce: It is reported that in Australia at least one in three marriages ends in divorce.

http://www.huffingtonpost.com.au/mark-mccrindle/is-australia-really-the-1_b_9129164.html - Mark McCrindle - Huffington Post - February 8, 2016

. Abuse & Neglect: In one year (2008-2009) there were over 200,000 were the subject of one or more child protection notifications.

http://www.aihw.gov.au/publication-detail/?id=6442468325 -Aust Govt. Institute of Health & Welfare. 2008-2009

. **Sexual Abuse:** According to reports one in four girls and one in six boys is sexually abused before they reach the age of 18. Of course this figure could be higher as many cases go unreported.
http://nctsn.org/nctsn_assets/pdfs/caring/ChildSexualAbuseFactSheet.pdf - referenced on link

This has to be one of the worst possible things that can happen to a child. A child does not have the capacity to deal with that kind of offense and it is NOT their fault.

. **Bullying:** Another huge problem is bullying. Bullying can come in several forms: Teasing, physical harm, harassment or even isolation. This can occur in schools, the workplace or in cyberspace, etc. Bullying of any kind can be devastating to the victim and can lead to depression and other mental health issues. It can even lead to suicide. It's important to remember that bullying is not the behaviour of a normal, well-adjusted person. Accurate figures on bullying are not attainable as unfortunately, many cases go unreported. However, if a person is suffering from bullying, in any form, it is important that they reach out for help. Reaching out does not indicate weakness; rather it shows great inner strength.

. **Grief:** Many people may suffer from grief of some form or other, including the loss of someone or something precious. The loss of health, a job, a sibling, a parent, a spouse, friends, financial loss, etc.

Once again, no accurate recordable figures are available on this, as much goes unreported.

. **Depression or Anxiety:** We have huge rates of depression and anxiety in this nation and there can be numerous contributing factors or circumstances.

. **Domestic violence:** Again the real figure is unattainable as an unknown number of cases go unreported.

The following is a quote from an organisation called ANROWS - (Australia's National Research Organisation for Women's Safety Limited) : May 14, 2014

"The information is drawn largely from the 2012 Australian Bureau of Statistics Personal Safety Survey. It shows that one in three women have experienced physical violence since the age of fifteen, while one in five have experienced sexual violence. The perpetrators of violence against women and violence against men are overwhelmingly men."

This is a shocking indication of the state of family life in this country and as stated earlier well over 60% of these cases are alcohol or other drug related.

I would hope that these figures would cause people to stop and think long and hard about this situation and how they can avoid any such behaviour in their own lives.

Acknowledgements

My ever loving Mum and Dad who went through more than any parent should have to because of my stupid choices. Who have also helped with editing not only this book, but the thousands of emails I have composed over recent years.

My brothers David and Ian for their prayers and love and help with my 'cause'.

My amazing teams of doctors, nurses, Professors and specialists, who not only used all of their brilliance and expertise, all those years ago, but also treated me with dignity and respect, despite my crazy behaviour.

My wonderful friends, Judy Young, Trish Taylor, Carolyn Hastings, Ros Mills and Rosalyn Dyne for their friendship and wonderful editing skills.

All of my close friends who have endured my random ravings as I have relived all of these wild memories.

Michael Davies, my publisher, for his wonderful assistance and patience throughout this process.

And last but not least, my three beautiful children, Kyle, Stefan and Phoebe, for just being the people they were created to be.

Presentations

In 2010 a secondary school teacher who knew of Kerryn's story, invited her to speak of her experiences to the Year 10 students in the school where he taught. Using her natural and honest manner, Kerryn's compelling message connected immediately with her audience. Her message was so well received by both students and staff, that it became the catalyst for her transition into the role of 'School Drug & Alcohol Awareness Educator'; fulfilling her passion to educate and warn others on the dangers of alcohol and other drug use and abuse.

While still carrying the physical scars from her past, for over seven years Kerryn has delivered her informative, engaging and highly regarded presentation to senior school students, corporate functions and to many other interested groups in various settings across Australia. She has also been involved in media interviews, forums on ICE and other drugs and featured in an SBS documentary on Marijuana.

Kerryn's message is not purely academic as she regularly receives calls from distraught parents who have a son or daughter who is battling drug or alcohol addiction. She has met with several of these people of varying ages and helped to guide some of them into rehabilitation facilities with some great outcomes.

With all of her experience and knowledge, Kerryn is passionate about educating people of all ages on the reality of drug and alcohol use and addiction and she is working hard in this field.

Kerryn is available to bring her very relevant and compelling presentation to senior school students, workplace meetings or corporate functions at: www.daesy.com.au under the 'Presentations' link.

Or by contacting Adrian from Speakers Solutions at:

adrian@speakerssolutions.com.au

Student Feedback

QUESTION... *"What message did you personally take away from the presentation?"....*

"Wow, Kerryn is so inspirational. Thanks for sharing!" Year 12 Student – Independent Co-educational College

"Kerryn was fantastic. She spoke with genuine honesty, and explained a difficult topic to us in a way that made it relevant." – Year 12 Student – Independent Co-educational College.

"I took away what drugs can really do with a personal story, instead of just watching a video, or listening to your basic lecture about the negatives of it." – Yr 9 Student – Independent Boys' Grammar.

"It reinforced just how dangerous drugs can be. Thank you, sincerely. I've never taken drugs but I have been exposed to them quite a fair bit. I started to think that perhaps taking drugs was ok. But it's not. So thank you for telling me that it's not." – VCE Student – Independent Ladies College.

"Drugs destroy lives & ruin relationships with friends, family & partners. Drug related deaths are so tragic. Have a dream/goal to reach in life." – Year 8 Student – Co-educational Catholic College.

"I thought it was incredibly insightful to hear from someone who has had first-hand experience. The different consequences from real life stories were very confronting, but necessary to hear. – VCE Student – Independent Ladies College.

"I loved the extra message of hope and having dreams, etc. – that was really nice to hear! Thank you! xx – VCE Student – Independent Ladies College.

"That alcohol can actually be very dangerous, especially when mixed with other drugs. Year 10 Student – Co-educational Government College.

"I'm glad you're alive to change other's lives." – VCAL Student- Narre Community Learning Centre.

"How much it can affect the people around you. Best presentation we've had! Thank you. :)" – Yr 12 student – Independent Girls' School.

"Don't do drugs at all & never binge drink or drink alcohol in large quantities. Always look out for your friends." – Yr 10 Student – Independent Co-educational College.

"I didn't realise that alcohol was as bad as drugs." – Yr 12 Student – Independent Girls' School.

"It really was an amazing presentation which has firmed up my views a lot, so thank you!" – Yr 12 student – Independent Girls' School.

"I really liked your talk better than other drug talks because of the personal stories." – Yr 12 student – Independent Girls' School.

"That the risk and dangers can be life threatening and how different someone can change because of it." – Yr 10 Student – Independent Co-educational College.

"That taking drugs isn't an escape route for things we can't handle." Year 8 Student – Co-educational Catholic College.

"The presentation was well organised and presented. Which was extremely informative, warning us about the effects and dangers of using drugs." – Yr 9 Student – Independent Boys' Grammar.

"That I will never do drugs and I learnt how to deal with someone overdosing." – Yr 12 Student – Independent Girls' College.

*" *Don't do Drugs. *You can do anything you set your mind to. VERY INSPIRATIONAL. "* – Yr 8 Student – Independent Catholic College.

"The full extent of the danger drugs and alcohol pose to society. It was a really great presentation. Thank you very much." – Yr 12 Student – Independent Girls' School.

"I never had the appeal to take drugs or smoke, but it has made me aware of the problems with peer-pressure and so I will be more cautious." – Yr 12 Student – Independent Girls' School.

Reference 1

17th January 2015

To whom it may concern

I have known Kerryn Redpath for over two years. I first met her through a friend, who arranged for Kerryn to meet with one of my relatives who was dealing with an addiction. We had tried to get some help for this family member without much success. After Kerryn met with him, he decided to go to rehab. As a result, he is doing remarkably well today.

Kerryn has a passion for people. Whenever I have spent time with her I have seen qualities such as non-judgmental acceptance of all people, kindness, genuineness, and an amazing ability to connect with people from all different walks of life.

While studying recently, I went to one of Kerryn's presentations at a college in late 2014. She spoke to a group of secondary school students. She has a natural ability to connect with the students and not only educate them on the dangers of experimenting with drugs and alcohol, but she threads her own personal story of her past addiction into the presentation. I watched students listen to her presentation and could see on their faces the profound impact of her words. It is one thing for young people to be educated about the danger of drugs but when it's coming from somebody who has personally struggled with addiction and lived to tell about it, students want to listen.

Kerryn's message is powerful. She has helped many people through her story and she is doing an amazing work in helping towards winning the war on drugs. I highly recommend Kerryn as a speaker. Her presentation is invaluable. Schools, community Organisations - all of us in the community would benefit from hearing one of Kerryn's presentations which will help spread the message that drugs destroy lives.

Sincerely,

J. A.

Graduate Cert. in Counselling AIFC, Cert. IV AOD

Reference II

Kerryn was recently invited to the organisation in which I work to deliver her important message on the topic of drug and alcohol related substance abuse and its impacts within the community and the workplace.

Kerryn delivered 12 highly personable and powerful presentations on the impacts of drugs and alcohol to employees over a 5 day period that struck a chord with many of the individuals present.

Kerryn is a remarkable speaker and very well educated on the subject of drug use/abuse in the workplace and in general.

I would highly recommend having Kerryn come speak with employees, students and the community. She did an incredible job of communicating the dangers of substance abuse and how it affects not only the addict but family members as well.

Kirsten Shepherd
HR Superintendent
Resources/manufacturing industry.
QLD

COMMENT ON DRUG EDUCATION

- Vic. Asst. Police Commissioner

"There needs to be work done in the community to tackle the demand for drugs. Their (drug cartels) tactics are to increase addiction and we need to educate people on the harms drugs do in the community". …. Victoria Police Assistant Commissioner, Stephen Fontana.

Big News - July 6-19, 2017. Edition 14, Vol 3.

www.bignews.com.au

CONTACT LIST FOR DRUG & ALCOHOL AND OTHER RELATED ISSUES

DIRECT LINE - Addiction Services
24 Hour Phone Counselling & Referrals & Extensive Services Data Base
Ph: 1800 888 236
Web: www.health.vic.gov.au/aod/directline.htm
Web: www.directline.org.au

LIFELINE
Crisis Support and Suicide Prevention
Ph: 131114
Web: https://www.lifeline.org.au/

ADF - HELP & SUPPORT - Alcohol & Drug Foundation
24/7, counselling, information and referral
Ph: 1300 85 85 84
Web: www.adf.org.au/help-support/

YOUTH SUPPORT & ADVOCACY SERVICE (YSAS)
Detox Service & Outreach service – Dandenong/Frankston
Ph: 1800 458 685
Web: www.ysas.org.au

THE BRIDGE PROGRAM
The Basin Centre – Salvation Army
Residential Recovery Program for Alcohol &Drug Addiction
Ph: 03 9762 1166
Web: www.salvationarmy.org.au

KIDS HELP LINE
Ph: 1800 55 1800 (Over 25 yrs - **Lifeline Ph:** 13 11 14)
Email: counsellor@kidshelp.com.au
Web: www.kidshelp.com.au

BEYOND BLUE
Depression & Anxiety Support Service
Ph: 1300 224 636
Web: www.beyondblue.org.au

YOUTH BEYOND BLUE
Ph: 1300 224 636
Email: bb@beyondblue.org.au
Web: www.beyondblue.org.au

HEADSPACE
Mental health issues/Depression/Anxiety
Ph: 03 9027-0100
Web: www.headspace.org.au

NATIONAL ALCOHOL AND OTHER DRUG HOTLINE
Ph: 1800 250 015
www.drughelp.gov.au

---

www.ingramcontent.com/pod-product-compliance
Lightning Source LLC
Chambersburg PA
CBHW050626300426
44112CB00012B/1682